CHILD DEVELOPMENT FOR TEACHERS

Sara Miller McCune founded SAGE Publishing in 1965 to support the dissemination of usable knowledge and educate a global community. SAGE publishes more than 1000 journals and over 800 new books each year, spanning a wide range of subject areas. Our growing selection of library products includes archives, data, case studies and video. SAGE remains majority owned by our founder and after her lifetime will become owned by a charitable trust that secures the company's continued independence.

Los Angeles | London | New Delhi | Singapore | Washington DC | Melbourne

CHILD
DEVELOPMENT
FOR TEACHERS

SEAN MACBLAIN

Learning Matters
An imprint of SAGE Publications Ltd
1 Oliver's Yard
55 City Road
London EC1Y 1SP

SAGE Publications Inc.
2455 Teller Road
Thousand Oaks, California 91320

SAGE Publications India Pvt Ltd
B 1/I 1 Mohan Cooperative Industrial Area
Mathura Road
New Delhi 110 044

SAGE Publications Asia-Pacific Pte Ltd
3 Church Street
#10-04 Samsung Hub
Singapore 049483

© Sean MacBlain 2020

First published in 2020

Editor: Amy Thornton
Senior project editor: Chris Marke
Project management: Swales & Willis Ltd, Exeter,
Devon
Marketing manager: Dilhara Attygalle
Cover design: Wendy Scott
Typeset by: C&M Digitals (P) Ltd, Chennai, India
Printed in the UK

Library of Congress Control Number: 2019946420

British Library Cataloguing in Publication data

A catalogue record for this book is available from
the British Library

ISBN 978-1-5264-6941-0
ISBN 978-1-5264-6940-3 (pbk)

At SAGE we take sustainability seriously. Most of our products are printed in the UK using responsibly sourced
papers and boards. When we print overseas we ensure sustainable papers are used as measured by the
PREPS grading system. We undertake an annual audit to monitor our sustainability.

For my brothers and our sister Louisa

CONTENTS

ABOUT THE AUTHOR

Professor Sean MacBlain PhD is an internationally recognised author whose publications include: *Learning Theories for Early Years Practice* (MacBlain, SAGE, 2018); *Contemporary Childhood* (MacBlain, Dunn and Luke, SAGE, 2017); *Dyslexia, Literacy and Inclusion: Child-Centred Perspectives* (MacBlain, Long and Dunn, SAGE, 2015); *Learning Theories in Childhood* (2nd edn) (Gray and MacBlain, SAGE, 2015); and *How Children Learn* (MacBlain, SAGE, 2014). Sean is currently a senior academic at the University of St Mark & St John, Plymouth, England, where he has held the positions of Research Lead for the Centre for Professional and Educational Research, Research Coordinator for the School of Education and Deputy Chair of the Ethics Committee. Sean worked previously as a Senior Lecturer in Education and Developmental Psychology at Stranmillis University College, Queen's University Belfast. He has taught in primary and secondary schools and in further education, and for many years worked as an educational psychologist. In addition to this, Sean also worked as a specialist dyslexia tutor when employed by Millfield School. Sean is married to Angela and lives in Somerset, England.

FOREWORD

Quite simply, teachers need to understand, appreciate and empathise with children and their development. The very essence of the profession relies on teachers adapting to children in a learning environment; the stories, the emotions, the dispositions and even the prejudices and expectations they bring. Teachers need to wrestle with what *childhood* means and how this meaning can change. However, this is far from easy. Learning and development are messy, both for children and teachers. This book is the guide for any trainee's development; the book that trainee teachers will want to return to in moments of reflection.

The design and organisation of the book recognises that teachers' development, just like children's, is not a linear process. As such, while the book can be read from cover to cover, each chapter has a clear theme that enables the reader to move directly to specific sections and ideas if they wish. The supportive design of each chapter encourages the reader to reflect, blending theoretical perspectives with case studies to bring the theories to life, and urging the reader to challenge themselves through discussion points, activities and further reading. The author clearly appreciates that in a profession that can face rapid changes in policy, it is imperative that every teacher is able to reflect on what is negotiable and non-negotiable in their professional lives. The author therefore does not promote the superiority of any one theoretical perspective over another, but subtly provides a framework to support the reader in drawing their own conclusions.

The book is comprehensive, stimulating and thought-provoking, encouraging the reader to challenge current understanding of children's development. The author provides a clear context for this challenge, notes the importance of giving children a voice in society, and emphasises how popularised assumptions of childhood and children's development need to be confronted. While these can be difficult issues, the style and feel of the text is both supportive and reassuring. For me, this is what is so special about this book – it addresses all the complexities associated with understanding children's cognitive, social and emotional development, but does so with warmth, depth and accessibility. Teachers will return to it, and I would thoroughly recommend it to anyone who is passionate about education.

Professor Ian Luke PhD PFHEA
Executive Dean
Plymouth Marjon University

ACKNOWLEDGEMENTS

I would like to offer my sincere thanks to Amy Thornton, whose vision created the idea for this text and who from the outset provided a most wonderful, valuable and critical sounding board – thank you, Amy. My thanks must also go to Amy's colleagues at SAGE who so skilfully guided this text through to production.

I must also pay tribute to our children's children, whose development I have observed and enjoyed while writing this book and who inspired me almost daily, and to my dear friend Barbara Hendon who has been so willing to share her vast experience and expertise in the field of child development. Finally, I wish to thank my wife Angela for her continued love and support throughout.

INTRODUCTION

To create effective learning environments teachers need to have a good understanding of their children's development, abilities, skills and interests.

(Palaiologou, 2019, p104)

Even in the months before birth, every child will have commenced a developmental journey that is unique only to them. From the moment of birth, they will then rely on support and guidance in most everything they do, first from their parents and primary caregivers, then from practitioners in early years settings, and later from their teachers. They will need support and guidance from adults because their development will unfold in ways they have yet to understand and because they will encounter unseen barriers that present challenges of varying magnitude. Being able to support and guide children's development as they progress along this unique journey is perhaps one of the most rewarding of professional experiences. Recently, Carter and Nutbrown (2014) encapsulated the joy that professionals involved in children's development and learning can experience as follows:

Children's learning is so complex, so rich, so fascinating, so varied, so surprising and so full of enthusiasm that to see it taking place every day, before one's very eyes is one of the greatest privileges.

(p129)

Trainee teachers have all of this to look forward to.

THE AIMS OF THE BOOK

The primary aim of this book is to inform trainee teachers of the importance of understanding how children's cognitive, social and emotional development impact on their learning. From the outset, it is recognised that no two children develop or learn in the same way. As trainee teachers read through this book, they may from time to time look back at their own schooling and reflect on how some of their teachers supported them with aspects of their own cognitive, social and emotional development, and how this impacted on their learning.

Children live differently today, and the life experiences they have as they grow through childhood will, in many ways, be very different to those their teachers experienced during their childhoods. Just over a decade ago, Sorin (2005) cited Steinberg and Kincheloe (2004), challenging us to confront the proposition that 'Children no longer live in the secret garden of childhood' and that children today 'possess an open door to the adult world' (p12). Our future teachers need to be trained to understand how children's development in a rapidly changing world impacts on learning and future academic achievement; this will require them to understand, among other things, the nature of childhood today, the changing shape of families, the impact of digital technology and social media on development, and the importance of good mental health and well-being.

CHALLENGES TO OUR UNDERSTANDING OF CHILDREN'S DEVELOPMENT

Popularised perceptions of children's development have in recent years been radically challenged as disturbing reports have appeared in the media concerning child neglect and abuse, issues around mental health and drugs, poverty, early sexualisation and commercialisation of children, and the impact of social media. The notion that all children grow up in stable and loving families has been increasingly recognised as false, with a growing recognition that significant numbers of children grow up in dysfunctional and even neglectful families where their development is adversely impacted upon by poverty and neglect, and in some cases abuse. To properly understand children's development and their social, emotional and academic needs, we must ensure that children's views are given a proper focus when we attempt to consider how they develop. Children's voices can in fact add a great deal to our understanding of their development and what it is to be a child today.

THE ORGANISATION OF THE BOOK

This text is organised in such a way that it offers readers a comprehensive account of child development and how development impacts on learning in a variety of ways. The text is set out in such a way that it offers trainee teachers discrete but complementary chapters, making it possible to read the whole text from beginning to end or to delve into individual sections as and when the need arises (e.g. when being asked to undertake a written assignment, give a presentation or explain the individual needs of children being taught while on placement).

Chapter 1 explores the nature of development and how different interpretations of development by philosophers, theorists and practitioners have sought to inform thinking and practice over generations. The link between development and learning is also explored, with particular emphasis given to starting school. Impending challenges for trainee teachers are also highlighted, and the importance of children having a voice in terms of their own development is addressed.

Chapter 2 explains why trainee teachers need to learn about children's development and why and how all children develop in unique and individual ways. The notion of 'readiness' for starting primary school is also addressed in detail, and is followed by a section on 'understanding the growing child', which looks at key milestones in children's development at Key Stage 1 and Key Stage 2. The issue of personality in children's development is also addressed in this chapter, as well as the importance of teachers becoming reflective practitioners.

Chapter 3 then explores cognitive development in children by explaining what cognitive development looks like and the influence of Jean Piaget before examining the important differences between *ability* and *attainment*. Language is also discussed in this chapter together with the emerging field of neuroscience and its contribution to our understanding of children's intellectual development.

Chapter 4 examines social development in children and how this impacts on their learning. The chapter explains what social development looks like and addresses the important element of moral development in children before looking at how environment shapes development and learning in children. The important issue of *self-efficacy* is examined in detail before looking at social fears that growing children might experience and the impact of these on development and learning. Transitions are also examined in this chapter.

Chapter 5 looks at the importance of emotional development and well-being in children and how this impacts on their learning. The chapter explains what emotional development looks like in Key Stage 1 and Key Stage 2 before looking at potential barriers to emotional development and well-being. The importance of *emotional intelligence* for children's learning is examined while also addressing the importance of teachers viewing children as *holistic learners*. Mental health is also discussed in this chapter, as well as the importance of *resilience* on children's well-being.

Chapter 6 examines how development in children is shaped by their behaviours and the behaviours of significant others in their lives. It focuses on the importance of trainee teachers understanding what is meant by the term *behaviour* and the importance of describing and recording behaviours in children in an accurate and precise manner. This chapter examines the principles underpinning the *behaviourist* approach to understanding and explaining children's learning, and looks particularly at *conduct disorders* in children, which impact greatly on their development and learning.

Chapter 7 examines the need for trainee teachers to learn how to make accurate assessments of children's abilities, attainments and potential and to implement purposeful and effective interventions. A range of case studies are described to support readers in understanding the *concepts* being put forward in this chapter.

Chapter 8 finally focuses on challenges facing trainee teachers in the future, such as issues to do with diet and nutrition, over-sexualisation, materialism and digital technology, all of which impact on children's development and learning, and in ways that are not yet fully understood. Trainee teachers are being prepared for a profession that is constantly changing and that is subject to political, economic and social forces and ideologies that at times seem to appear from nowhere.

Links to websites and YouTube videos are offered to readers throughout the text, alongside 'critical questions' to stimulate and enhance reflections and 'activities' as a means of promoting engagement by readers with their peers. Chapters contain case studies through which trainee teachers can see the relevance of the points being made by the author. Reflecting the author's own theoretical approach, the text will not promote the superiority of any one theoretical perspective; rather, trainee teachers will be supported and encouraged in forming their own conclusions by being introduced to appropriate and extended references and discussion points.

HOW READERS CAN GET THE BEST FROM THE BOOK

Though this text can be read from beginning to end, it should also be viewed as a valuable resource. A first reading of the entire text will help readers locate key aspects that are relevant to their own practice. Readers will find that they want to return to the text as they progress in their training and are faced with completing written assignments, giving presentations, and of course successfully completing placements in schools, all of which will be important for meeting the requirements of Qualified Teaching Status (QTS).

By way of introduction to the following chapters, it is worth reflecting upon the following from Rose and Wood (2016), who summarised children's development and the skills needed by those successful trainee teachers entering the profession as follows:

> *Children's development is not a case of following a linear pattern of learning. It should be viewed holistically ... The skills of the teacher are to identify the particular needs of the individual children and to support their learning, whilst offering appropriate challenges.*

(p101)

Each chapter clearly sets out its aims, and details what the reader can expect. This will be helpful to students working on assignments as well as those seeking to inform themselves about particular aspects of children's development.

Each chapter contains sections that focus on different theoretical perspectives. This is in addition to relevant Case Studies that relate theory to practice. Again, this will be very helpful for trainees tasked with completing assignments.

Each chapter clearly sets out its aims and details what the reader can expect. This will be helpful to trainee teachers working on assignments as well as those seeking to inform themselves about particular aspects of children's development.

Each chapter directs the reader to examples of further and extended reading as well as links to online sources. Discussion points and activities are also included to assist readers in working with fellow students on critical and challenging issues.

1

UNDERSTANDING DEVELOPMENT

WHY YOU SHOULD READ THIS CHAPTER

Children's development and learning go hand in hand. Some years ago, Gray and MacBlain (2015) emphasised the importance of this connection when they indicated how:

> learning precedes birth. Brain development begins three weeks after conception. From the 30th week of gestation the neural architecture, sometimes referred to as wiring or hard wired, that supports the learning process is in place.

> (p11)

More recently, Rose and Wood (2016) stressed the importance of teachers understanding that brain development is a crucial feature in children's learning, and not just in their early years, but importantly throughout their primary years and beyond:

> The brain has the capacity to grow and learn throughout our life time but is most responsive during childhood, particularly in the early years, with connection density peaking just before puberty.

> (p87)

Following birth, children continually interact in a multitude of ways with those around them, and while much of their learning is incidental, much is also directed by adults. The role that adults play in guiding and shaping children's development and learning increases significantly as children's educational experiences move increasingly from their homes into early years settings and then primary school. Trainee teachers need to understand, therefore, that each child they teach will have commenced a unique learning journey that began before they were born and that is being constantly shaped by a multitude of factors, one of which will be the way they manage their learning. To properly know one's pupils then requires that trainee teachers recognise, appreciate and understand how their pupils' individual development has brought them to that point where they then begin to teach them.

By the end of this chapter, you should know:

- what characterises development in children;

- how development underpins learning;

- the importance of theory;

- how explanations of children's development have differed over generations;

- that teachers will face new challenges that are emerging because of changing patterns in childhood;

- why children should be given a voice; and

- how to relate children's development to the UK QTS standards.

INTRODUCTION

The importance of trainee teachers having a sound knowledge of children's development and under-standing how a range of issues in their lives can affect development and subsequent learning has been recognised for some time. More recently, the *Carter Review of Initial Teacher Training* (Carter, 2015) felt it necessary, however, to emphasise that 'In order to teach effectively, trainees need to understand typi-cal expectations of children at different stages of development' (p9). Importantly, the *Carter Review* also recommended that 'Child and adolescent development should be included within a framework for ITT [initial teacher training] content' (p9). It is the author's contention, having worked as a primary and secondary teacher, and later as an educational psychologist for over 20 years and as an academic researching in this area, that for teachers to properly address the learning needs of their pupils, they need to have a sound understanding of how children develop.

How children develop clearly affects their learning; when trainee teachers find themselves in the future making important decisions about their pupils' learning and academic progress, they must take proper account of prior social, emotional and cognitive factors. By doing so, they will then feel confident that they are addressing the individual needs of pupils and effectively supporting them in realising their potential. It is also the author's contention that trainee teachers need to develop their skills in critically appraising the learning environments they encounter when on school placements, and recognise that the individualised nature of each school will impact differently on the course of development in each child; as part of this process, they also need to reflect on what types of school environment they think contribute to progressive development and effective learning.

Following their training, newly qualified teachers (NQTs) should also be encouraged to take time to revisit and critically engage with elements of their training, in particular how theory can support them in understanding the wide range of developmental issues they encounter. The importance of drawing upon theory was clearly emphasised some years ago by Bigge and Shermis (2004) as follows:

> teachers without a strong theoretical orientation inescapably make little more than busy-work assign-ments. True, some teachers operate in this way and use only a hodge-podge of methods without theoretical orientation. However, this muddled kind of teaching undoubtedly is responsible for many of the current adverse criticisms of public education.

(p5)

Importantly, Bigge and Shermis (2004) went on to emphasise how:

> teachers who do not make use of a systematic body of theory in their day-to-day decisions are behaving blindly; little evidence of long-range rationale, purpose, or plan is observable in their teaching.

(p5)

Since then, there have been major advances in the content of initial training courses, which have in part addressed this issue; there remains, however, a wide variation in the extent to which this takes place in practice.

CHILDREN ARE GROWING UP DIFFERENTLY

Popularised notions of children's development have been radically challenged in recent decades as disturbing reports have appeared in the media concerning child neglect and abuse, issues around mental health and drugs, increased austerity and poverty, early sexualisation and commercialisation, and the growth in social media. The idea that all children grow up in stable and loving families has also been increasingly challenged, as a growing recognition emerges of significant numbers of children being born into dysfunctional, neglectful and even abusive families.

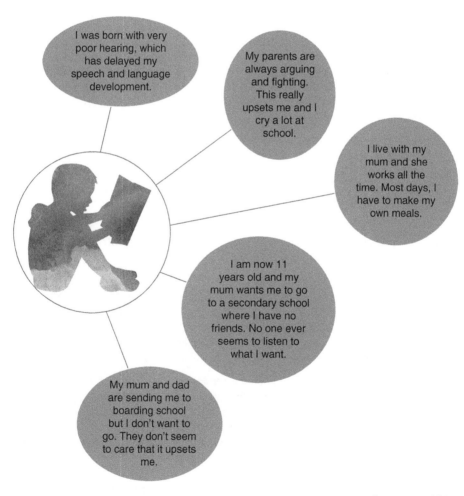

Figure 1.1 Children's lives

CHILDREN'S VOICES

To properly understand children's development, therefore, and more particularly their social and emotional needs and well-being, we need to ensure that children themselves are given a voice, and importantly are listened to. It is now well accepted that children's voices, when heard, add much to our understanding of development, and importantly what it is like being a child today (Dunn, 2015; Lundy, 2007; Lundy and McEvoy, 2009; Lundy et al., 2011).

▬ CASE STUDY 1.1 ▬▬▬▬▬▬▬▬▬▬▬▬▬▬▬▬▬▬▬▬▬

Recognising differences in development

Sara has just completed her training and has begun working with a class of 28 children in Key Stage 2, in a local primary school that has recently been rated by Ofsted as 'Good'. She takes time to read previously written notes on five of her pupils, which include the following:

Jenny was very young when she contracted meningitis, which resulted in significant hearing loss; as a result, she has had difficulties with language development and this has affected her acquisition of literacy, in particular learning the sounds of letters. Spelling has been very challenging for Jenny. She has become increasingly withdrawn and is frequently excluded by other children from their games. When in the classroom, Jenny needs to sit at the front of the class to hear her teachers, and from time to time she has been teased by the others, and on occasions even mimicked.

Suzy comes to school most days looking quite upset. Her mother has refused to speak with teachers about the home situation and has even refused to attend meetings with the head teachers. The family is known to social services, and Suzy has confided many times to her previous learning support assistant that her father often hits her mother and that she hides away in the home when her father loses his temper, especially when he has been drinking.

James lives alone with his mother who is a single parent. Most days when James returns from school, he has to prepare all of the food for the evening meal. His mother works shifts and sometimes has to work late into the night. This has been the normal pattern of home life for James since he started primary school.

Since starting primary school, Lucie's mother and father have insisted that she spends at least an hour every morning before coming to school studying. She also has extra tuition after school three times per week. Her parents want her to attend a grammar school many miles away, and feel that a grammar school education will compensate for Lucie's lack of time with other children in her own community.

Oscar is a happy child and popular with the other children. He is very able and loves school. His father has recently been appointed to a new job overseas, and his parents have taken him to view a number of independent schools in different parts of the country where he will board when they move abroad to take up his father's new job. Oscar is very upset, and desperately wants to go to the local secondary school with his friends and remain living in the area, but his parents have stressed that this is impossible. Most days, he comes to school quite upset.

Because this is her first teaching position, Sara is keen to do well. She arranges to meet with the deputy head teacher to talk about these children because she feels, from reading their notes, that she will have to deal with aspects of their emotional and social development that are clearly impacting on their learning. She also reflects on her training when tutors emphasised the importance of understanding how events in the lives of children can affect their development and subsequent learning. Having talked with the deputy head teacher, she arranges to meet with each of the five children's parents to try to develop a working relationship with them, which she hopes will help her to talk openly with them about her concerns. All parents are happy to do so, and Sara then sets aside some time each week to talk individually with each of the five children and build a relationship with them, which would enable them to open up about any anxieties they might have. As the months go by, Sara realises that she has not only built a good relationship with each of the five children, but she has also done so with their parents, who have been able to provide her with a wealth of information about their child's early development; in this way, she has gained a much fuller understanding of the children, which has also led to a greater understanding of the type of learning environments that best support them in their learning.

This case illustrates how a range of factors can impact on children's development; it also exemplifies the importance of trainee teachers recognising that they will be teaching children whose personal backgrounds will have already impacted hugely on their development, and therefore their learning.

EXPLAINING DEVELOPMENT

We know that from their earliest days, children display characteristic and distinctive behavioural patterns that not only reflect individual learning, but also brain development. Take, for example, the way in which children acquire and develop movement. While newly born infants have only a relatively small number of movements, these movements do not simply occur in some arbitrary and indiscriminate way, but have a purpose; they are, in a sense, predetermined, as they offer the means by which infants can begin to make sense of the world around them. In a very short time, following birth, they will acquire behaviours that are directed towards achieving particular ends, an example of which would be their first movements, which gradually lead to them being able to sit up, crawl, and then walk and run. Learning is therefore well underway by the time children are ready to enter more formalised education. Teachers in primary and even post-primary schools need to fully appreciate that many of the patterns of learning they observe in pupils and how their pupils think will have had their origins in those first crucial years following birth.

How children develop as they grow from birth and through childhood and adolescence has long exercised the minds of philosophers, theorists and practitioners, and has led to many contrasting explanations. Having different explanations should not, however, be seen as problematic, but instead should be viewed as an enriching process that offers an eclectic array of options. To fully appreciate the complex nature of children's development, trainee teachers need to engage with different theoretical perspectives that have sought to explain development in children and that have, over the years, informed and shaped practice in schools. Not all qualified teachers, however, have engaged in this process, as was suggested less than a decade ago by Jarvis (2005), who proposed that:

> *Education differs from comparable professions, such as medicine and psychology, in that although there is a thriving field of professional research, it takes place largely in isolation from professional practice ... teachers largely ignore education research.*

(p204)

Since then, there have been significant advances in educational research and practice, resulting in a more informed body of teachers who now, as part of their training and ongoing professional development, are required to source and understand research within their field, and importantly revisit those theories that have underpinned their practice.

THE NEED FOR THEORY

In their simplest form, theories are a means of explaining complex phenomena that we do not fully understand (MacBlain, 2019). Some students who embark on professional training courses for working with children, however, still need to be convinced of the importance of theory. Recently, Walsh, in the foreword to MacBlain (2018), encapsulated this as follows:

As a teacher educator, I am often confronted with a response of apathy when I introduce students, particularly those in the initial years of their degree programme, to any form of theoretical issue or philosophical debate. Familiar comments include: … 'it is only when I am in the classroom that I really learn – all this theoretical stuff is just a waste of time'. These students appear only interested in the everyday practices of the classroom context and fail to appreciate [how] … we need to look at notable philosophies and theorists to help us unravel and deconstruct our own understandings.

(p8)

Walsh went even further, citing McMillan (2009), who argued that:

an ability to reflect on appropriate theories is essential to equip students to become competent professionals … Failing to embrace these theoretical issues may result in what could be described as narrow and shallow perceptions of what constitutes high quality practice … which Walsh (2017) suggests will do little to address the real learning needs and interests of the young child.

(MacBlain, 2018, p8)

No single theory can properly explain the complexity of children's development and learning (MacBlain, 2019); different theories do, nonetheless, complement each other, and in doing so add significantly to our understanding. Recently, Rose and Wood (2016) indicated how conflicting theoretical positions might confuse teachers attempting to understand how development impacts on their pupils' learning as follows: 'when theory appears to provide conflicting arguments about what this role should entail' (pp99–100). They have illustrated this by comparing how the role of adults working with children has been explained by Piaget, Bruner and Vygotsky, and by more recent research in the field of neuroscience:

With his [Piaget's] emphasis on children as individual learners … the implication is that the adult role is largely to provide a suitable context for exploration, allowing the child to develop at their own natural pace. However, a Piagetian approach neglects the importance of negotiation and collaboration in learning. The work of Bruner, Vygotsky and from neuroscience emphasises the social and cultural context as being intrinsic to learning and gives the adult a more pivotal and proactive role in determining the advancement of children's learning.

(Rose and Wood, 2016, pp99–100)

Rose and Wood (2016) have advised practitioners to take a 'consilience' approach, which they suggest 'attempts to draw together different perspectives' (p100). Of equal relevance is the fact that having a good understanding of different theoretical approaches provides teachers with the means by which they can engage with colleagues about pupils' learning and explain elements of their learning in ways that show they are informed, as opposed to being only able to offer simplistic descriptions and vague interpretations of learning that would not stand up to proper scrutiny.

USING THEORY TO THINK ABOUT YOUR PRACTICE

Trainee teachers will encounter practice while on placement that has been informed by different theoretical approaches to managing children's learning. These approaches will have emerged gradually over decades and even generations as new insights into children's development have informed thinking. Most, if not all, practice will have its origins in the ideas of philosophers, theorists, thinkers and practitioners. An example of the influence of theory on practice can be found in the fact that much of the education in the UK following the Second World War was dominated by *behaviourism*, a theoretical approach that sought to explain children's learning largely in terms of their responses to stimuli presented by teachers. The result of adopting this approach meant that much of children's learning was reduced to receiving facts from teachers and responding to closed questions. Recently, Gray and MacBlain (2015) encapsulated the *behaviourist* approach to children's learning as follows:

> For almost fifty years, behaviourism … remained a dominant force in education. Classroom teaching was based on rote and drill (involving the repetition of times tables, spellings etc.) in the belief that this would promote learning. Using these approaches, teachers could test children's memory for facts such as the letters of the alphabet, colours, spelling and multiplication tables.
>
> (p65)

Behaviourism came to be challenged, however, by other theorists such as Piaget, Dewey and Bruner, who viewed children's development differently and rejected what they saw as the *behaviourists'* overly simplistic way of explaining learning in terms of stimuli and responses. Instead, they chose to look more at internal cognitive processes that they believed underpinned children's thinking and that could not be directly observed. Gray and MacBlain have illustrated the strength of Piaget's criticism of *behaviourism* (Piaget, 1952), where he argued that 'it merely encouraged the repetition of "meaningless strings" and "circus tricks" but failed to promote understanding' (Gray and MacBlain, 2015, p65). Buckler and Castle (2014) have also emphasised how theorists such as Piaget and Bruner had rejected the principles of *behaviourism* and focused more on the internal and unseen workings of the brain (i.e. children's cognitive processing):

> Whereas the brain was not important in the observation-laden approach of behaviourism, the cognitive perspective placed the brain, or rather its functions, firmly at the centre of human behaviour … The cognitive perspective emphasises the importance of explaining behaviour in terms of internal events, the meaning of concepts and processes, beliefs, attitudes and intentions.
>
> (p18)

Buckler and Castle (2014) have gone on to stress how the emerging field of *cognitive psychology* had explained 'cognitions' as 'thoughts, language, memory, decision-making, attention and information processing – that inform our everyday lives' (p19), which were, some would argue, largely ignored by the early *behaviourists*. It is not uncommon to find teachers whose practice is influenced by a combination of different theories; often this is done, however, without a full understanding of the core principles that underpin the theories.

CRITICAL QUESTION

How might knowledge of different theoretical perspectives support you in reflecting on the learning you have observed on school placement?

CONNECTING DEVELOPMENT TO LEARNING

Our understanding of how children's development underpins learning at different ages remains limited. We now know that the course of development is unique to each child and that social, emotional, cognitive and physical factors play a significant role in children's learning. Indeed, it is only in recent decades that the complex dynamic of environmental and biological factors that underpin children's development, and therefore their learning, has begun to be properly acknowledged and researched with real purpose (MacBlain, 2014; MacBlain et al., 2017).

INTERPRETING CHILD DEVELOPMENT: PREDOMINATING LEGACIES

Why and how children develop in the ways they do is still not fully understood. Theoretical approaches, as we have seen, have in the past offered different descriptions and explanations of development and have sought to influence the thinking and practice of teachers (MacBlain, 2014, 2018). Though each theoretical approach has been challenged in one way or another, some continue to influence thinking and practice. Some years ago, Daniels and Shumow (2002) emphasised how some theoretical approaches have dominated thinking and practice in previous decades when they suggested that:

> *actual educational practice throughout this time period has been modelled on conceptions of learning and development defined by the behaviourist tradition (Brown, 1994) or by extreme biological views such as entity ideas that intelligence is fixed or maturationist views that children develop on their own.*

(pp496–7)

Daniels and Shumow (2002) have gone on to stress how in more recent years, some psychologists have 'denounced those prevailing beliefs and practices' that have been a legacy from the past, with the result that 'attention has been refocused on "child-centred" practices, identified with constructivist, social constructivist, or ecological theories' (p496). Importantly, they also recognise that while 'some conceive of the differences among theories as irreconcilable (Case, 1998), others see them as complementary (Cobb, 1994)' (p497). They also remind us that:

Common threads relevant to education among these theorists include the ideas that effective teaching must be based on understanding the child and the vision of children as active agents in their own education.

(p497)

To better understand those attempts that have been made at explaining children's development and learning, it is useful to now look more closely at differing theoretical legacies that have influenced and even dominated thinking and practice. We begin by looking at the ideas of some of the early philosophers and thinkers, which, though formed generations ago, nevertheless continue to influence how we perceive development and learning today.

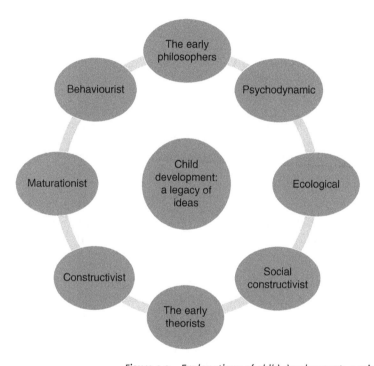

Figure 1.2   Explanations of child development: a mixture of legacies

EARLY PHILOSOPHERS AND THINKERS

Early philosophers, such as John Locke (1632–1704), Jean-Jacques Rousseau (1712–1778), Johann Pestalozzi (1746–1827) and Friedrich Froebel (1782–1852), viewed childhood as a special time when children needed nurturing from adults and opportunities to grow as children. They viewed children as unique individuals and saw play and freedom of expression as key aspects of childhood, which are ideas that are central to practice today. Their ideas were radical and presented enormous challenges to the thinking of their time, when children were largely viewed as 'small adults' and the *concept* of childhood often not even recognised. Today, many early years practitioners and primary teachers still look to the ideas of these early philosophers as being important influences in the legacy of practice they have inherited.

LATER THEORISTS AND THINKERS

Later theorists and thinkers, such as Sigmund Freud (1856–1939), Rudolf Steiner (1861–1925), Maria Montessori (1870–1952) and John Dewey (1859–1952), established principles that they believed would explain children's development and learning. Many of their ideas remain embedded in practice today. Montessori's ideas, for example, continue to inform thinking and practice today, as evidenced by the number of Montessori settings throughout the world.

▬ KEY THEORY

Montessori's legacy

Montessori originally devised the notion of 'planes', or stages through which children pass. During the first 'plane', children experience change in social, emotional and physical development, and between 2 and 6 demonstrate a natural interest in music, displaying a 'refinement of the senses', imitating the behaviours of adults. Around 3 to 4, they display an interest in sensory stimuli, such as taste and touch, and writing and copying written symbols, such as letters and words. Between 3 and 5, interest is shown in the sounds that letters make and how written words are spoken. During the second 'plane', thinking becomes more abstract.

We now look at a number of theoretical approaches that have sought to explain children's development and learning, and begin with those that have emanated from the original work of Sigmund Freud, the father of psychodynamic theory.

The *psychodynamic* view of child development continues to influence thinking and practice today, and particularly in therapeutic settings. This approach has its origins in the theoretical ideas of Sigmund Freud and his followers (for more detail of Freud's theory, see Chapter 5), where teachers actively support children in understanding their inner feelings and emotions, and take time to understand tensions that children at different ages and stages of development might be experiencing. Play is viewed as a means by which children can work through emotionally problematic experiences while being able to feel safe within a secure environment. An example of this approach can be located in the early work of Susan Isaacs (1885–1948) with preschool and 'nursery' children.

▬ KEY THEORY

Isaac's legacy

Having worked as an educationalist, Isaacs entered the field of psychoanalysis, believing that central to children's development was their need to develop inner feelings and emotions. She saw learning environments as important resources in allowing children to externalise and manage difficult emotions, emphasising the benefits of teachers getting into children's worlds but not impeding natural thinking.

A more recent example of Freud's influence can be found in the work of Alexander Sutherland Neill (1883–1973), who is perhaps best known for his radical views on education and the unique school he founded, Summerhill, which remains open today. Neill's views on learning were strongly located within the field of psychodynamics, and he is associated with providing learning environments where children are free to learn and where there is very little adult control.

▬ KEY THEORY

Neill's legacy

Freud's influence on Neill can be seen in his book *Summerhill*:

> *Freud showed that every neurosis is founded on sex repression. I said, 'I'll have a school in which there will be no sex repression'. Freud said that the unconscious was infinitely more important and more powerful than the conscious. I said, 'In my school we won't censure, punish, moralize. We will allow every child to live according to his deep impulses … a child is innately wise and realistic. If left to himself without adult suggestion of any kind, he will develop as far as he is capable of developing …'. In regard to his school, Summerhill, 'lessons are optional … Children can go to them or stay away from them – for years if they want to'.*

(Neill, 1968, p20)

▬ CRITICAL QUESTION

Visit the website for Neill's school, Summerhill: **www.summerhillschool.co.uk**. What might trainee teachers gain in regard to meeting the QTS standards if on placement at Summerhill?

Behaviourists viewed development in children in terms of behaviours that are reinforced, with the view that associations develop between stimuli and responses, which account for all learning. They proposed that learning could be observed and explained in a systematic and objective manner through observation and experiment (a much fuller discussion of *behaviourism* comes later in Chapter 5).

Maturationist views tend towards viewing children as developing by themselves. Daniels and Shumow (2002) have indicated how this approach to explaining child development places particular emphasis on children's innate knowledge and their disposition to move naturally through stages, coupled with inherent tendencies to explore the worlds into which they are born. Teachers, Daniels and Shumow (2002) suggest, who base their teaching on this approach, which can be located in many Montessori early years settings, create learning environments and offer activities that address 'stage-related developmental needs'; these teachers maintain a 'relatively passive role, only "interfering" with children's self-directed activity on occasion' (p504).

Constructivist views of child development find agreement among child-centred approaches where children as they develop are seen as active participants in learning and as responding well to activities that are creative and motivating for the child and that incorporate problem-solving as a key element in learning.

Social constructivist views of development, such as those that have their origins in the work of Vygotsky (1978), advocate for the notion that as children develop, their thinking and learning is essentially a product of their social experiences, interactions with others, and those cultural tools they encounter in their lives such as fairy stories, nursery rhymes and art. In addition, this approach emphasises the importance of children having opportunities as they grow up 'to solve problems with adult guidance or in collaboration with more skilled peers', as opposed to having to engage in such activities by themselves (Daniels and Shumow, 2002, p507).

Ecological views of development, such as those found in the work of Bronfenbrenner (1979), emphasise 'the importance of the settings and circumstances' in which children grow and develop. Teachers will therefore be influenced in how they teach by the social contexts in which their pupils are living and have grown up. Drawing upon the work of Heath (1983) and Moll and Greenberg (1988), Daniels and Shumow (2002) have indicated how the ecological approach can guide teachers in directing their pupils' learning by 'understanding how the knowledge, practices, and language socialization patterns within children's families and communities contribute to children's ability to function in the classroom' (p498).

CHAPTER SUMMARY

- The role that teachers play in guiding and shaping children's development is crucial to their learning.

- Trainee teachers need to understand that the pupils they will be teaching will have commenced unique learning journeys that commenced even before they were born.

- To understand children's learning needs, teachers need to recognise and appreciate how individual development has brought them to the point where they begin to teach them.

- Trainee teachers need to have a sound grasp of what characterises development in children and how development links to and underpins learning.

- Children should be encouraged to have a voice.

EXTENDED READING

Daniels, D.H. and Shumow, L. (2002) 'Child development and classroom teaching: a review of the literature and implications for educating teachers', *Applied Developmental Psychology*, 23: 495–526. This research paper offers a comprehensive and accessible account of how teaching impacts on child development.

Gray, C. and MacBlain, S.F. (2015) *Learning Theories in Childhood* (2nd edn). London: SAGE. A very accessible and comprehensive text that provides many insights into key theories and how these can support teachers in understanding children's development and learning.

2

WHY TRAINEE TEACHERS NEED TO KNOW ABOUT CHILD DEVELOPMENT

WHY YOU SHOULD READ THIS CHAPTER

Trainee teachers need to know about children's development for many reasons. Every child they encounter as teachers will bring to each learning situation innate dispositions, individualised biographies and accumulated histories of learning. These will all have been shaped in their homes and preschool settings and will be characterised by patterns of behaviour that are often difficult to understand and not always predictable. They will present with different personality traits, emotional and social strengths and vulnerabilities, and likes and dislikes; importantly, they will also have expectations, which, though they are unable to articulate, will mean that they need their teachers to be empathetic towards them and support them in reaching the potential they have been born with, and that is rightfully theirs.

By the end of this chapter, you should know:

- why trainee teachers need to understand the nature of children's development;

- how development at different ages can impact on learning;

- how children develop differently;

- whether or not development occurs in stages;

- what constitutes readiness to begin primary schooling;

- why it is important to observe aspects of development in pupils;

- that Key Stage 1 teachers play a major role in children's development when they begin school and in preparing them for later development in Key Stages 2, 3 and 4; and

- how trainee teachers can relate children's development to their training in meeting the QTS standards.

INTRODUCTION

The importance of teachers knowing about child development is clearly evidenced throughout the literature (Buckler and Castle, 2014; Crowley, 2014; Rose and Wood, 2016). Daniels and Shumow (2002) have, for example, emphasised how 'taking a developmental perspective means attempting to perceive the world from the child's perspective' (p518). They further cite the work of Olson and

Bruner (1996, pp12–13), who, in their studies of the educational practices employed by teachers and their belief systems about children and about their learning and knowledge, state that 'the first step in "equipping" teachers (or parents) for their task is to provide them access to the best available understanding of the mind of the child' (Daniels and Shumow, 2002, p498).

Understanding the minds of individual children also requires that teachers have a sound knowledge of their development. The importance of teachers knowing about child development is also clearly evidenced within the standards set out for Qualified Teaching Status (QTS) in the UK (DfE, 2012). Children grow up in families, communities, cultures and societies that differ in a multitude of ways. Circumstances at birth will vary enormously and children's lives will be shaped not only by those around them, but also by their physical environments and the dispositions they have inherited. Trainee teachers need to be mindful, therefore, that when they begin their professional careers as teachers, each class they take will be made up of a set of young minds, all of whom will have been influenced by the complex interplay between their biologies and the world around them. Their needs as learners will therefore be very individualised and very different.

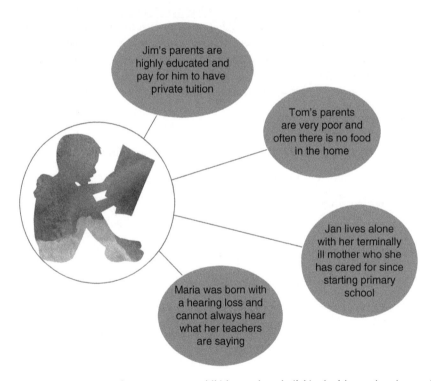

Figure 2.1   Every child is a unique individual with an abundance of potential

DEVELOPMENTAL READINESS

While most children embrace the move to primary school, there will be some who will not, and they may find the whole experience immensely challenging and even frightening. Much will depend on how they have been prepared for this transition and how the receiving primary school welcomes and supports them. In the UK, children enter formal education in the year they are 5, by which time their development has already been considerable. From this point, the day-to-day opportunities they have to engage in learning activities and the quality of support and direction they are given will be largely dependent on the decisions made by their teachers. Children, as we have seen, develop at very different rates, and no two children starting primary school will have reached the same levels of development; importantly, their internalised patterns of learning will also vary enormously. For these reasons, it is essential that trainee teachers fully understand that children starting school will learn differently and will have already had much of their thinking and approaches to learning shaped by significant others. The role of the teacher, then, in children's first years of primary school will be to build on what children have already learned and create environments that support future development through Key Stages 2, 3 and 4, and into adulthood.

BACKGROUND MATTERS: IDENTIFYING THE STARTING POINTS

A survey by Ofsted (2014a) entitled *Are You Ready? Good Practice in School Readiness* revealed that for many preschool children growing up in deprived areas, educational failure begins even before they attend primary school, with 'gaps in achievement between the poorest children and their better-off counterparts' being 'clearly established by the age of five years', evidenced by 'strong associations between a child's social background and their readiness for school as measured by their scores on entry into Year 1'. A key reason for this was a 'lack of firm grounding in the key skills of communication, language, literacy and mathematics'. Ofsted offered the following cautionary note: 'Too few who start school behind their peers catch up by the time they leave education', though some providers in areas of high deprivation 'buck the trend' by quickly identifying 'children's starting points' and using 'discrete adult-led teaching sessions as part of a range of provision to accelerate progress'.

Finding • We found various views on the definition of school readiness and whether the term refers to readiness to start school on entry to Year 1 or at the start of entry into Reception.

Finding • Evidence of good practice in engaging parents and carers was seen mainly but not exclusively through children's centres. They were particularly effective in working with other agencies to engage vulnerable parents and target support where it was most needed.

Finding • We found examples of very good practice where providers in disadvantaged areas worked closely with parents and carers through the transition period. These providers were increasing parental understanding of what was expected in terms of school readiness and were providing parents with information and guidance on how best to get their child ready.

Figure 2.2 Selected findings from Ofsted (2014a)

Importantly, Ofsted's survey also revealed how some children fail to 'make rapid enough progress because far too many settings pass on unreliable assessments. Too often, time is lost through unreliable and inaccurate assessment, time that cannot be regained'. Ofsted concluded that this was in part due to there being 'no nationally set baseline, which defines school readiness'. Several Ofsted findings are offered in Figure 2.2.

THE RECEPTION YEAR

Most parents choose to start their children in primary school in the Reception Year, which is commonly referred to as the first year of school, though, unlike other years of schooling, it is not compulsory. Children entering a Reception class will vary enormously in their development and will require a level of expertise from their teachers that incorporates a sound knowledge and understanding of social, emotional and intellectual development. This, however, has been found not to be the case. Recently, in January 2017, Her Majesty's Chief Inspector (HMCI) commissioned an Ofsted-wide review of the curriculum, with its primary aim being to offer 'fresh insight into leaders' curriculum intentions, how these are implemented and the impact on outcomes for pupils' (Ofsted, 2017). The review offered a focus on the Reception Year and the extent to which a school's curriculum for 4- and 5-year-olds was preparing them for their future education. The review emphasised how the Reception Year in primary schools should be seen, as holding 'a unique and important position in education' and as marking 'a significant milestone in a child's life'. Importantly, the review also emphasised how 'For parents, it is the end of early education and care … and the start of school'. Given the importance with which the Reception Year is viewed, it needs to be reported that the review offered the following rather worrying finding:

> For too many children, the Reception Year is far from successful. It is a false start and may predispose them to years of catching up rather than forging ahead. In 2016, around one third of children did not have the essential knowledge and understanding they needed to reach a good level of development.

Importantly, the review offered the following explanation of what a 'good' level of development was as follows:

> A child achieves a good level of development, as defined by the government, if she or he meets the expected level in the early learning goals in the prime areas of learning (personal, social and emotional development; physical development; and communication and language) and in the specific areas of literacy and mathematics by the age of five.

This notion of what a 'good' level of development is remains open to question when one considers the outcomes for disadvantaged children.

CRITICAL QUESTION

Given that many theorists and philosophers believe development up to age 7 should be supported through play, then should measurements of a 'good level of development' include children's attainments in 'the specific areas of literacy and mathematics by the age of five'?

UNDERSTANDING THE GROWING CHILD

As teachers take on a new class, it is important for them to get to know their pupils and to fully understand that there will be significant differences in the development of each pupil, which will have already impacted significantly on how they have learned in the past and how they will learn in the future. Some children in Key Stage 1, for example, may be experiencing difficulties with following instructions, have limited vocabulary, and display poor listening skills and deficits in attention caused by a delay in their acquisition of language; by contrast, others may be very advanced in their language and have already acquired an extensive vocabulary, good verbal comprehension, and strong abilities in focusing and sustaining attention. Some will be more physically developed than their peers and some will be emotionally very stable, having benefited from lots of love, attention and nurturing from their families and significant others. Readers may wish to reflect on the varying levels of ability they themselves observed in those children with whom they shared a classroom when attending primary school.

Children develop physically, intellectually, socially and emotionally in very different ways. A child may, for example, be developing physically at a far more accelerated rate than they are emotionally. Equally, a child who is developing their intellectual skills and abilities at a very fast rate may remain physically immature for some years and be overtaken in height by many of their peers. The implications for learning of uneven development are many, and how teachers manage children's learning as they move through the primary and post-primary years will be extremely important; variations in development across a class of 30 children will be enormous, not to mention the issue of summer-born children who, it needs to be recognised, will be chronologically much younger than many of their peers.

Children need to learn the norms and values expected of them by society; this may not have happened prior to commencing school, and some parents may have even worked against this process by creating within their home alternative norms and values that fall well short of what is expected outside of the home and in school. Many children, as they grow, will require support with managing

- What are the expectations for each pupil?

- What developmental levels have pupils achieved?

- Have any of the children experienced emotional trauma in previous years, such as the death of a parent?

- Do any pupils live in a dysfunctional family?

- Given the different levels of development of pupils, how much time should be allocated to different aspects of the curriculum?

- If a significant number of pupils struggle with literacy, how much additional time should be given to this at the expense of other aspects of the curriculum?

Figure 2.3   Helpful questions for focusing on pupils' development and learning

feelings and emotions that they do not understand; crucially, they will also be dependent upon their teachers having accurate knowledge of their intellectual development and acquired strengths and weaknesses in order that they receive learning experiences that are appropriate for their individual needs. Figure 2.3 suggests some questions that trainee teachers can use as a focus during their school placements as a means of considering how individual levels of development impact on the learning of their pupils and how they themselves might think about adjusting aspects of their teaching.

PHYSICAL MILESTONES

Physical development in young children not only involves actual growth of their bodies, but also brain and motor development, and importantly the development of fine motor skills that will be needed later for writing, drawing and manipulating apparatus. As children grow, their visual and hearing abilities also mature; this aspect of their sensory development is clearly very important for their learning and crucial for the acquisition of literacy. Children who have problems with hearing in Key Stage 1 may, for example, experience difficulties with phonological processing, resulting in early problems with word recognition and spelling. Equally, children who have visual processing problems may experience difficulties with tracking words across the pages of their reading books, meaning that for these children reading can become a laborious and even confusing process for them. The result of these delays and/or difficulties in physical maturation may mean that for some children, they fail to embrace the excitement of reading and writing, and most worryingly of all are perceived by their teachers and their peers as slow learners when in fact the nature of their difficulties are of a physical nature.

KEY STAGE 1

5-YEAR-OLDS

Children entering primary school at 5 years of age are becoming better coordinated with greater precision in many of their physical actions and a growth in their ability to balance. Typically, they will be losing fatty tissue and will be developing muscle capacity; teachers will observe marked growth spurts in some children at this age, though not in others. Most will be able to dress and wash themselves, use buttons and in some cases tie shoelaces; they will mostly be able to use the toilet independently. Teachers will observe children at this age being able to hop and skip, with their capacity to run being now quite well developed. They will be able to bend and touch their toes while not bending their knees.

Playtimes can become very energetic and even boisterous. Though they are learning to use scooters, ride bicycles with stabilisers and skip using ropes, their understanding of the rules required to participate in games such as football and rounders will be limited, and even beyond some of them. They are still learning to use knives and forks with dexterity, cut up their food, use and apply manners, converse socially with other children during mealtimes, and take turns with things. Their fine motor skills will also be developing, as evidenced by being able to count the fingers of one hand using a finger from their other hand, having greater control when holding pencils or crayons, and completing jigsaw puzzles and threading beads on a string, as well as drawing a picture of a person that includes legs, eyes, a mouth and a nose.

6-YEAR-OLDS

Children now vary quite a lot in their physical abilities, and some will have started to demonstrate a natural ability in some sports (e.g. in their precision with throwing and catching a ball, as well as running and jumping). They will be able to skip in time to music, jump off apparatus in the gymnasium and ride a two-wheel bicycle without stabilisers. Some will be growing very quickly and at a much faster rate than others in their class. They will appear to have endless energy and will be losing more of their fatty tissue and developing more muscle. Coordination is becoming more refined and precise as gross and fine motor skills develop; this will be apparent in their ability to play group games as well as games that demand greater skill; they will be acquiring a much better understanding of the rules of games, as well as the need to have rules and to abide by these. While physical skills and abilities may appear to be developing at a fast rate in some children, in others this may appear to be taking more time. By this age, most children will have progressed their drawing skills and be able to use tools needed for creative activities, such as scissors and paintbrushes. They will be able to hold their pencils as adults do and write their first name and surname (providing it is not immensely complex).

KEY STAGE 2

7-YEAR-OLDS

At this age, motor skills are developing further, and children can achieve much greater accuracy when attempting activities that require more careful movement and dexterity. This will be noticeable in the playground and during physical education (PE) lessons, and of course with handwriting and the manipulation of objects in craft, design and technology. Most can ride a two-wheel bicycle without stabilisers and without support, and do so with a high level of precision, managing to swerve and not crash into others or physical objects; they will also demonstrate increased interest in creating their own physical games and activities with their friends. They will be skilful at throwing and catching a ball and will be able to do this using only one hand. They will display much greater stamina as with running and swimming. They may also be observed to show increasing signs of being more competitive with their peers. Better fine motor skills will enable them to draw pictures of people that include greater detail, such as fingers, toes and clothes. Their skills with writing will be more advanced so that they can accurately write individual letters with clearer differences between upper- and lower-case letters.

8-YEAR-OLDS

Teachers will observe increased physical abilities and skills in their pupils at this age, and some may be showing signs of being much more interested in their own bodies and how they appear to others. As coordination improves, children typically rejoice in excelling in physical activities and games and may even want to show off at the expense of others. Fine motor coordination is now much improved, and some children may be developing their abilities to play musical instruments and to draw with much greater accuracy. Throwing and catching will be very much improved and stamina will be greater, with some children able to demonstrate an ability to run for quite long distances. Limited activity at this age can, however, lead to becoming overweight and, in more pronounced cases, obesity.

9-YEAR-OLDS

Children are now drawing closer to adolescence and puberty, when they will begin to experience quite marked changes in their own physical presence and that of their peers. This can create significant issues for some children. Girls typically commence puberty between 8 and 12 years of age, and boys between 9 and 14 years of age. Some children, therefore, will experience the early stages of puberty at this age. Motor skills are improving and physical strength is greater, and most children can now attend to their own personal hygiene without support from adults. Parental influence remains strong, and parental attitudes to diet, exercise and activity will continue to be a strong influence.

10- AND 11-YEAR-OLDS

Children are nearing completion of primary school and some may already be thinking of themselves as being like older children; this may particularly be the case with 11-year-olds who mix with older children outside of their school or who have older siblings. Some 10- and 11-year-olds begin to show signs of adolescence, while others will not until they are in their first years of secondary school. Such variations may cause discomfort for some children who may be overly sensitive to their own appearance, and especially how they appear to the opposite sex. Growth spurts are common at this age, and teachers working with this age range will become quickly aware of the increased variations in height of their pupils.

LANGUAGE MILESTONES

Trainee teachers preparing to work in primary schools should know how language develops and understand how language development and cognitive development are interrelated and dependent on each other. On school placements, trainee teachers should take time to discuss with class teachers and with teachers with responsibility for language development what their schools do to promote good language development and what steps they take to work with children experiencing difficulties in this area. While all teachers are aware of the important function that language plays in the learning of young children, it is, however, crucial that they also recognise the important role that written language plays in language development.

THE ROLE THAT WRITING PLAYS IN LANGUAGE DEVELOPMENT

It is through written language that children are most typically challenged to demonstrate their learning while at school. This was most eloquently demonstrated some decades ago by one of the author's professors, Brown (1977), who offered the following observations:

> Before the child can write or read he must be able to identify the symbols and the sounds they represent. Evidence suggests that visual recognition may be possible quite early, but that the association of the symbol with a sound, a cross-modal link between vision and auditory discrimination, may take longer. For written language the child must also have a high degree of motor coordination.

(p119)

A further and very important consideration emphasised by Bruner (1975) is that the cognitive structures of children who have been actively encouraged to engage with written activities while at the same time engaging with reading activities will typically be different. Drawing upon the work of Bruner, Brown (1977) again commented as follows:

> He [Bruner] suggested that the mind of a person who spent much of his time in these activities might be 'profoundly different' from that of one who was involved in non-linguistic activities such as drawing or building, and perhaps even different from that of one who mostly talked and listened. He suggested that there may be a minimal use of language in ordinary discourse which has little effect upon an individual's thought patterns, but beyond that level it may transform them. The most important step in this transformation he saw as instigated by the transference from speech into some form of notation such as writing or mathematical symbols. In this form it becomes more powerful. The rules which must be obeyed to construct written sentences may allow some people to analyse the products of their thoughts and to operate with formal operations (Piaget's term) in ways which would not otherwise be possible.
>
> (p119)

Clearly, such a view has important implications for practice in primary schools. This also comes at a time when schools in the UK are finding themselves being faced increasingly with a growing perception in government that children should be introduced to more formal pedagogies involving writing and reading, even in their preschool years. Such concerns were recognised some years ago by Miller and Pound (2011), who commented as follows:

> External pressures from government guidance or a management hierarchy can lead practitioners to focus on curriculum 'delivery' or 'coverage' as the main focus of their practice. Such a view would have been anathema to the foundational theorists ... but in England it has become a feature of the Early Years Foundation Stage (EYFS) (DfES, 2008) and the National Curriculum in primary schools, causing uncertainty for many practitioners.
>
> (p165)

Though the debate continues as to the nature of the pedagogies in the learning of children in the early years, it is important to understand that stimulating spoken language alongside reading and writing, even in its most basic forms such as making marks and symbols, should continue to receive serious consideration by teachers in primary schools.

LANGUAGE AS A MEANS OF EXPRESSING EMOTIONS AND FEELINGS

It should also be recognised that language is at the core of social and emotional development in children, who from their first days and weeks use language as a means of gaining attention from others around them in order to be fed, to be played with and to be nurtured. Most infants are competent in communicating with others and having their basic needs met, long before they have learned words and phrases; in fact, we now know that children are already programmed at birth to acquire language and then develop this through stages of acquisition. For some children growing up in homes where spoken language is limited to shouting, their abilities to express feelings and emotions through language may be adversely affected.

LANGUAGE DELAY

Sadly, it is the case that many children entering primary schools in the UK have language delay and very poor listening skills, a point that was brought to the public little more than a decade ago by Palmer (2006), who offered the following rather stark observation:

> *Everywhere I went it was the same story: four- and five-year-olds were coming to school with poorer language skills than ever before; they weren't arriving with the repertoire of nursery rhymes and songs little ones always used to know, and children of all ages found it increasingly difficult to sit down and listen to their teacher or to express complex ideas in speech or writing ... I also discovered that this issue was bothering teachers across the developed world.*

(p105)

Palmer's accounts are indeed disturbing and suggest that many children in the UK are failing to be supported in their development of language. While some children have poor experiences of language modelling in their homes, there will be other children who experience more specific difficulties. Children with dyspraxia and dyslexia, for example, may have problems with aspects of their language functioning, as will be the case for children with Asperger's syndrome; it is crucial, then, that teachers in primary schools are informed about the nature of language development and the types of difficulties that their pupils may experience so that correct interventions can take place, which in some instances may require referral to the speech and language therapy service.

In a recent briefing paper published on the internet, Save the Children (2018) reported that, 'One child in five starts primary school in England without the language skills they need to succeed, a figure that rises to one in three of the poorest children (DfE, 2015)' (p1). They indicated that the findings were based on an analysis of the Millennium Cohort Study that had been undertaken by the UCL Institute of Education for Save the Children, which examined the relationship between the language skills of children at 5 years of age when they enter school and their later attainments in English and mathematics at 7 years of age and then 11 years of age when they finish primary school. The analysis found that 1 in 4 children who struggled with language at 5 years of age failed to reach the expected standard in English at the end of primary school. This was compared with 1 in 25 children who had demonstrated good skills in language at 5 years of age.

The analysis also revealed how 1 in 5 children at 5 years of age who struggled with language failed to reach the expected standard in mathematics at the end of their primary schooling; this was compared with 1 child in 50 who demonstrated good skills in language when starting primary school at 5 years of age. The briefing paper by Save the Children (2018) went on to indicate that by 5 years of age, when children enter primary school, they should be capable of speaking in full sentences, using most of the everyday words used by adults, be asking lots of 'why?' questions to understand their world, and demonstrate an ability to talk with confidence about things and events that happened in the past and that might happen in the future. At 7 years of age, they should be able to:

> *Read and write independently, speak confidently, and listen to what others have to say. Count, read, write and order numbers to 100 and beyond, as well as develop a range of mental calculation skills; learn about space and shape; and start to understand mathematical language.*

(p4)

By 11 years of age, they should be able to:

Learn how to apply the way they speak and write to different contexts, purposes and audiences … be able to read a range of texts and understand different layers of meaning in texts, as well as explore the use of language in literary and non-literary texts … Move away from counting to calculating, trying to tackle problems with mental methods before any other approach; use measurement skills and a wide range of mathematical language, diagrams and charts to present their reasoning.

(p4)

Cowie (2012, p83) proposed four key areas of language that she suggests children and young people need to master (see Figure 2.4).

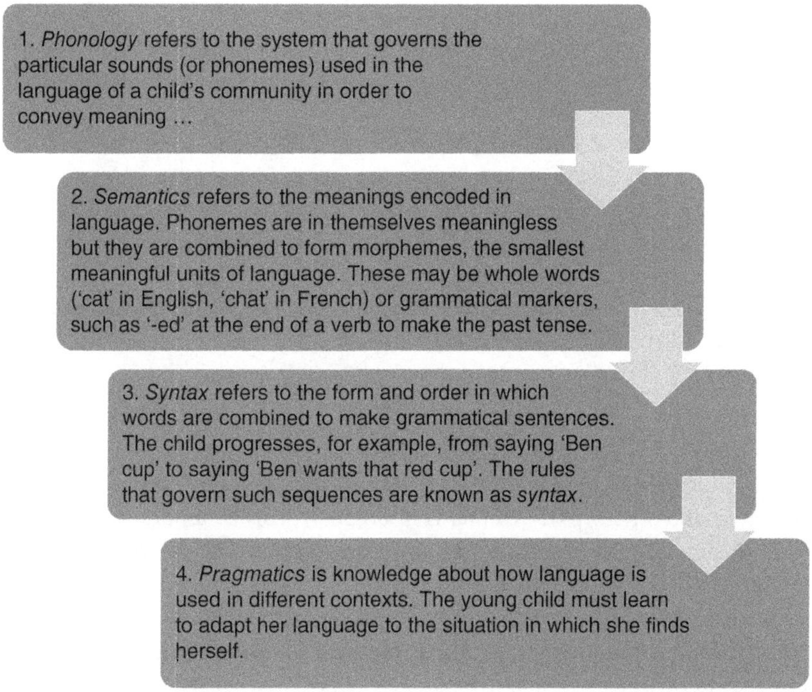

1. *Phonology* refers to the system that governs the particular sounds (or phonemes) used in the language of a child's community in order to convey meaning …

2. *Semantics* refers to the meanings encoded in language. Phonemes are in themselves meaningless but they are combined to form morphemes, the smallest meaningful units of language. These may be whole words ('cat' in English, 'chat' in French) or grammatical markers, such as '-ed' at the end of a verb to make the past tense.

3. *Syntax* refers to the form and order in which words are combined to make grammatical sentences. The child progresses, for example, from saying 'Ben cup' to saying 'Ben wants that red cup'. The rules that govern such sequences are known as *syntax*.

4. *Pragmatics* is knowledge about how language is used in different contexts. The young child must learn to adapt her language to the situation in which she finds herself.

Figure 2.4   Cowie's four key areas of language

PERSONALITY AND DEVELOPMENT

The term personality is a complex one and is so often used in a variety of vague ways to describe others. When used by professionals such as teachers, however, the meaning of the term needs to be clear, accurate and specific, and properly understood by the recipient; all too often, this term is used without much thought being given to what it means. It is not uncommon, for example, to hear such phrases as 'He's got a nice personality', 'I find her personality a bit strange', and so on. When discussing the personalities of pupils with other professionals and with parents, it is vital that trainee teachers learn to properly acknowledge the uniqueness of each child's development and use descriptions and explanations that are accurate and have meaning and can be shared and understood by those to whom they are talking to. Using descriptions to account for children's personalities that are vague, uninformed and lacking in accuracy and specificity can, in the long term, do children a huge disservice, and may even label children in ways that are detrimental to them.

In exploring personality development in children, Brown (1977) invited us some years ago to consider personality as 'a term which denotes a whole range of attributes', which individuals 'may be said to possess and which are manifest' in their 'modes of behaviour and thought' (p124). It is worth deconstructing Brown's explanation and looking closer at the words and phrases he uses. To begin, he uses the word 'term', and by doing so appears to be emphasising the importance of acknowledging that this complex aspect of children's development can be referred to by using an agreed verbal construct (i.e. the word 'term'). He then refers to 'attributes' that individuals 'may' possess; the process whereby individuals acquire attributes is a complex one, and can be understood in part by looking at how individuals attribute meaning to the behaviours of others. Some years ago, Gross (1992) explained this process of attribution as follows:

> *Most of our impressions of others are based on what they actually do – their overt behaviour – and the setting in which it occurs ... Sometimes ... our impressions may be based on second-hand information ... we usually try to explain why the person behaved as they did by identifying the cause of the behaviour ... was it something to do with the person, for instance, their motives, intentions or personality (an internal cause) or was it something to do with the situation, including some other person or some physical feature of the environment (an external cause) ... The process by which we make this judgement is called the attribution process.*

> (p473)

Gross (1992), however, raises a note of caution in regard to the *attribution* process: 'even though almost all behaviour is the product of *both* the person and the situation, our causal explanations tend to emphasize one or the other' (p479, emphasis in original). This is important as all too often teachers find themselves looking for the causes of undesired behaviours within a child and not paying enough attention to the environment. Take the example of a child in Key Stage 2 whose emotional development is delayed who thinks that behaving in a silly way makes him popular. His teacher may attribute the child's behaviours to naughtiness as opposed to really understanding that the environment, or more specifically the classroom dynamics (i.e. an *external* cause), are what is really driving the child's behaviours, and not just causes that are *internal* to the child, such as the child's immaturity in emotional development.

FOCUS ON THEORY

It is helpful when seeking to understand personality development to consider two quite different approaches, namely the *idiographic* and the *nomothetic*. The first of these emphasises the uniqueness of individuals, while the latter seeks to identify patterns in human behaviours commonly thought of as 'traits' and proposes that through studying patterns of behaviour or traits, it is possible to understand how personality develops. In essence, the work of Sigmund

Freud and subsequent psychodynamic theorists lies within the *idiographic* approach. Though controversial, Freud's contribution to our understanding of personality development has been substantial. Miller and Pound (2011) have, for example, emphasised how the legacy of ideas offered by followers of Freud, the *psychoanalysts*, have become 'embedded in the culture of the industrially developed world, including in relation to the development and care of children' (p22). Freud argued that central to personality development lie two determining elements characterised by *pleasure* and by *tensions*. He suggested that tensions arise from sexual energy (the libido) and that pleasure emanates from a release of this sexual energy – Freud employed the term 'sexual' in a broad sense to explain all thoughts and actions that are found pleasurable by individuals. Freud also believed that individuals move through a series of stages, the first of which is the oral stage (Figure 2.5).

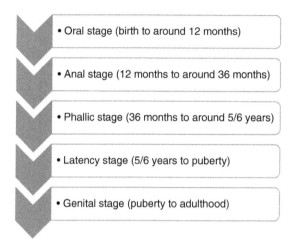

- Oral stage (birth to around 12 months)
- Anal stage (12 months to around 36 months)
- Phallic stage (36 months to around 5/6 years)
- Latency stage (5/6 years to puberty)
- Genital stage (puberty to adulthood)

Figure 2.5   Freud's stages of development

Oral stage (birth to around 12 months)

The personality is being shaped by the libido, which centres on the mouth. Children derive satisfaction through putting things in their mouths – they put objects in their mouths and they can also be observed sucking on objects they have to hand, this in addition to gaining satisfaction from breastfeeding or when feeding from a bottle. Freud proposed that overstimulation of children during this stage can in some cases result in children developing oral fixations later on in their lives, which might be manifested by behaviours such as thumb-sucking and smoking, which he further proposed might then become accentuated when individuals experience very high levels of stress later on in their lives.

Anal stage (12 months to around 36 months)

Freud proposed that at this stage, the libido has become more concentrated on the anus, with children experiencing pleasure when defecating. He believed that as children move into this stage, they have already begun to see themselves as individuals; a process of realisation has commenced, and children are now becoming more aware that their own needs, wishes and desires might conflict with

(Continued)

(Continued)

those of others. Excessive conflict encountered at this stage or having overly severe boundaries imposed upon them by adults may, he argued, define how children relate to authority in later lives and may even result in exaggerated and often unnecessary respect for authority. Insisting that children become potty-trained at too early a stage can, Freud suggested, result in them becoming adults who are anally retentive and with patterns of behaviour characterised by their need to be excessively clean. Freud also believed that conflict during the anal stage might result in children becoming overly stubborn and even miserly when they become adults.

Phallic stage (36 months to around 5/6 years)

During this stage, children's personality development is becoming increasingly centred around their genitals, with masturbation offering a new sense of pleasure. Children are now much more aware of the differences between the sexes, and it is this growing awareness that Freud believed can bring degrees of conflict in some children, which is typically manifested through physical attraction to others, but also such emotions as rivalry, jealousy and even fear. Freud referred to this process as the *Oedipus complex* in boys and the *Electra complex* in girls. Tensions at this stage, he believed, can become resolved as children gradually identify with parents of the same gender.

Latency stage (5/6 years to puberty)

As children enter and move through this stage, the libido ceases being active. Freud suggested that during this stage, sexual impulses become repressed, with the sexual energy of children being redirected towards external activities (e.g. sport and hobbies as well as peer friendships). Children's energies are also now being channelled into developing their knowledge and skills, and play with children of the same gender is becoming more evident.

Genital stage (puberty to adulthood)

The latency stage is followed by the genital stage when adolescence is beginning; this is often viewed as a time when young people form identities and engage in experimentation.

The following two case studies illustrate a number of the key principles underpinning the psychodynamic approach to understanding personality development in children.

■ CASE STUDY 2.1

Children's development and the importance of love

Zoe is 6 years of age and lives with her mother, who is a registered Class A drug user; Zoe has been neglected emotionally by her mother since birth and has never met her father. Most nights, she watches her mother getting high on drugs and consuming large quantities of alcohol. Most weekends, her mother goes out clubbing and to bars, returning in the early hours of the following morning. Zoe spends long periods of time alone. The family has been known to social services since a referral was made by the health visitor shortly after Zoe's birth. At nursery school, staff raised concerns with social services about Zoe's poor appearance and her general health and demeanour.

They were especially concerned that Zoe was very withdrawn and reluctant to play with others, preferring to remain with adults for most of the time and being extremely clingy and infantile. Her language and social skills were very delayed.

▬ CASE STUDY 2.2 ▬

Children's development and the importance of security

Charlie is 7 years of age and recently lost his mother following a long illness. His teacher spends time with Charlie talking about his mother. He finds this very calming and reassuring, even though it makes him cry. His teacher meets each week with Charlie's father and talks with him about any especially upsetting times he has observed with Charlie at home. In this way, the teacher feels she is not only offering support to Charlie, but also to his father. Charlie's father is very thankful that he is able to talk to Charlie's teacher and share any difficulties at home, such as Charlie's poor sleeping patterns and eating habits. He feels very reassured by such meetings, which in turn impacts very positively on Charlie.

A number of key figures have adapted Freud's ideas and have contributed much to our understanding of personality development in children. While much of Freud's original thinking and that of his followers is still celebrated and continues to influence practice, a number of criticisms have been levelled against it. A primary criticism is that many of Freud's original ideas are not empirically verifiable (i.e. they cannot be tested). How, for example, do we know that children move through such stages as the 'anal' or 'phallic' stages, and what do these stages actually look like? Are they, for instance, the same for every child? How sure are we that boys move through an 'Oedipus complex' and girls an 'Electra complex'?

DOES DEVELOPMENT OCCUR IN STAGES?

We so often hear others referring to stages of development in children; it is not uncommon, for example, to hear such phrases as 'he's passed that stage now' or 'she's going through a difficult stage', and so on. While these phrases are in common use, they are, in effect, often rather meaningless. There may be some form of popular agreement about what they might mean, but they lack specificity; they are too broad and too vague, and therefore of little real use to the practising teacher. The notion of 'stages' begs many questions. What, for example, constitutes a stage, how long is a stage, what are the characteristics of a stage, and are they the same in all cultures across the globe? Mercer (2018) cautions us when using the term 'stage' to think of it as a term that requires careful consideration. He has stressed, for example, how the *concept* of a 'stage' in child development is metaphorical, and as such requires 'that we should make careful use of it and not assume that stage ideas are necessarily good descriptions of how each child develops' (p35).

Whether children develop through stages is a question that has exercised theorists and philosophers for generations. There are those theorists, such as Piaget and Erikson, who view development as moving through stages, while others see development in terms of responses to environmental influences, such as those of the *behaviourist* tradition (see Chapter 5). Mercer (2018) has gone on to caution students about too readily using the *concept* of stages:

> *Students are often attracted to stage theories because they seem so complete and definite … However, like all metaphors, the stage concept is easily abused and can mislead us, so be warned!*

> (p35)

Importantly, Mercer (2018) emphasises how developmental stages are not the same as physical stages as they are not of a uniform length, and importantly 'are not necessarily linked to the chronological ages often associated with them' (p35). Developmental stages, she stresses, 'overlap each other' (p35), and older children may even choose to imitate earlier stages of their development.

OBSERVING DEVELOPMENT: BEING A REFLECTIVE PRACTITIONER

It has often surprised me (the author) how little time teachers give to observing individual children's learning behaviours; by this, I don't mean looking around the classroom to 'see' if all the children are engaged and on task, or 'watching' them while they engage in activities with others. What I mean here is the act of really looking carefully at the individual or micro-behaviours of children. To fully understand how development impacts on children's learning, teachers need to critically reflect on their pupils' learning in ways that demonstrate purpose and meaning (Hattie, 2008, 2012; Hattie and Yates, 2014; MacBlain, 2014). The process of reflection at a critical level has been well explained by Daudelin (1996, p39), cited in Zwozdiak-Myers (2007), who has suggested that:

> *reflection is the process of stepping back from an experience to ponder, carefully and persistently, its meaning to the self through the development of inferences: learning is the creation of meaning from past or current events that serves as a guide for future behaviour.*

> (pp160–1)

This explanation is helpful as it emphasises characteristics of best practice, namely 'stepping back', 'carefully and persistently', 'meaning', 'inferences' and 'behaviour'. These constructs offer teachers the means by which they can evaluate their practice; they also offer teachers the means by which they might reflect on the environments they put in place and shape for their children. They also offer teachers a means by which they can not only observe children's learning behaviours, but importantly how they can interpret their behaviours.

WHAT MAKES FOR GOOD OBSERVATION?

When one listens to good teachers talking about their own teaching, it quickly becomes very apparent that their conversations are characterised by a number of key factors: a definite sense of purpose in what they are asking of their pupils, a clarity in their understanding of the nature of the learning environments they have created and want to create, the individual needs of their pupils, and importantly how children at different developmental levels will be able to approach the tasks they are presenting and achieve some levels of success. Discussions between teachers about their pupils' learning are characterised by objectivity; they are focused and, importantly, largely evidence-based. Discussions of this type indicate deeper and more systematic understanding of the cognitive, emotional and social factors that drive the individual learning patterns of each pupil.

Effective teachers engage in purposeful observation and reflect carefully on the inferences they make about the behaviours they observe (MacBlain, 2014) and they listen carefully to what parents say about their children. They 'carefully and persistently' focus on behaviour patterns in their pupils, and particularly micro-behaviours, when children are working with their peers or have become absorbed in a particular activity that interests and motivates them. Purposeful observation, which leads to accurate interpretations of behaviours in different learning situations, will provide important information about intellectual development, as well as emotional and social development, and learning. Trainee teachers therefore need to develop their observation skills, as reflective and purposeful observation will inform their assessments and lead to effective interventions and future planning of learning activities. Commenting on the importance of observation, Nutbrown (2006b) has suggested that 'observation and assessment are the essential tools of watching and learning with which practitioners can both establish the progress that has already taken place and explore the future' (p99).

AFTER TRAINING: CONTINUING PROFESSIONAL DEVELOPMENT

Following their initial training, teachers entering the profession need to ensure that their schools provide effective continuing professional development; they should also be expected to further develop their knowledge base and skills. It has been the author's experience over many years working as an educational psychologist that too few teachers are given enough time out of their busy teaching schedules to reflect critically on how their pupils experience the learning environments they create, an observation that is also shared by others (Hattie, 2008, 2012; Hattie and Yates, 2014). It has also been the author's experience that too few teachers actively seek to update their practice by engaging with new research in the field (Jarvis, 2005). Teachers need to fully appreciate how children's learning is inextricably interwoven with their development; to properly address the individual learning needs of each pupil also requires teachers to properly understand their developmental needs.

CHAPTER SUMMARY

- Trainee teachers need to properly understand the nature of children's development because each child develops differently.

- Development at different ages impacts on learning.

- Development can be very different (e.g. physically and in language).

- School readiness is very important and impacts on learning.

- Teachers need to develop their observation skills.

- Trainee teachers need to know how to relate their knowledge of children's development to meeting the QTS standards.

━━━━━━━━━━ **EXTENDED READING** ━━━━━━━━━━

MacBlain, S.F. (2014) *How Children Learn.* London: SAGE. This is a very comprehensive text that covers most areas of learning in children from birth and through their school years. The text is accessible and offers a large number of useful examples.

Additional information on Sigmund Freud can be found at **www.freud.org.uk**

3

CHILDREN'S COGNITIVE DEVELOPMENT

WHY YOU SHOULD READ THIS CHAPTER

How children think and how they learn is complex. Trainee teachers need to understand that no two children think in the same way and that the nature of children's cognitive development is crucial to how they learn. While patterns of behaviour can be observed in how children approach different learning tasks, these do not in reality represent or explain the complexity of their underlying thinking processes; this is why teaching can be one of the most challenging but immensely rewarding of professions.

By the end of this chapter, you should know:

- what cognitive development in young children looks like;

- why it is important for trainee teachers to understand different theoretical approaches that explain children's thinking and learning;

- why it is important to differentiate between ability and attainment;

- how language shapes development and learning;

- the contribution neuroscience is making to our understanding of children's learning; and

- how cognitive development in children relates to the UK QTS standards.

INTRODUCTION

The nature of thinking in children is not yet fully understood. The main reason for this lies in the fact that every child thinks differently, and as they grow their thinking is influenced by a multitude of factors. We know, however, that as children develop, they internalise patterns of thinking that are unique and individual only to them, and that these individualised patterns of thinking shape their learning. While children entering primary school will display similarities in how they learn, it needs to be understood that how they approach learning tasks and activities will be qualitatively different and will reflect their individualised and unique levels of development; failure to properly acknowledge and understand the importance of prior development on children's learning can lead to misguided priorities and ineffective strategies, leading to failure. Over two decades ago, Fontana (1995) emphasised this crucial point when he stressed how:

some teachers are unclear of the level of thinking (or cognition) they can reasonably expect of a child at a given age. Much educational failure, indeed, stems from the fact that forms of thinking are demanded that children are incapable of applying.

(p51)

The importance of teachers' understanding how thinking and cognitive development impact on children's learning is now well accepted (Ofsted, 2010) and is embedded in the standards set out for Qualified Teaching Status (QTS) in the UK, where teachers need to:

LINKS TO TEACHER STANDARDS

- *be aware of pupils' capabilities and their prior knowledge, and plan teaching to build on these (A2);*

- *demonstrate knowledge and understanding of how pupils learn and how this impacts on teaching (A2);*

- *know when and how to differentiate appropriately, using approaches which enable pupils to be taught effectively (A2);*

- *demonstrate an awareness of the ... intellectual development of children, and know how to adapt teaching to support pupils' education at different stages of development (A5); and*

- *make use of formative and summative assessment to secure pupils' progress (A6).*

(DfE, 2012)

ACTIVITY

Before reading the next section, write down a definition of 'thinking' and a definition of 'learning', then consider how the two are different. Discuss your definitions with other trainee teachers and determine if you are in agreement, and if not, why not?

THE CONTRIBUTION OF JEAN PIAGET

COGNITIVE CONSTRUCTIVISM

One of the most ambitious and celebrated attempts made at understanding and explaining children's cognitive development was undertaken by Jean Piaget, who, though articulating his ideas some decades ago, nevertheless continues to influence thinking and practice even today. A key feature that needs to be fully grasped when seeking to understand Piaget's ideas on children's cognitive development, and how they construct their thoughts and the world around them, was articulated most eloquently by Rose and Wood (2016) when they drew attention to how 'Piaget argued that children are intrinsically motivated to learn and actively construct their own meaning, hence the term "constructivism"' (p95).

SCHEMAS: WHAT ARE THEY?

Piaget proposed that it is through interacting with the environments around them that children create within their brains internal mental representations, or structures, which he referred to as *schemas*. While this may appear to be a difficult *concept* to understand, it is not! Nutbrown (2006a) has offered the following most helpful means for understanding *schemas*, explaining these as 'a way of labelling children's consistent patterns of action' (p7). Trainee teachers will observe examples of consistent patterns of behaviour in pupils when on school placements; by taking time to observe *schemas*, they can familiarise themselves with how individual pupils engage in learning activities, what motivates them to learn, and what types of opportunities and environments best supports their learning.

SCHEMAS OR CONCEPTS?

While Nutbrown has offered a means of understanding *schemas*, it is also necessary to differentiate these from *concepts*. Some years ago, Hayes (1994) described *schemas* as being like cognitive maps that enable children to engage in activities such as planning, while *concepts*, on the other hand, enable children to classify phenomena such as objects they see and play with and events that occur around them (pp143–4). Fontana (1995) has emphasised how it is through *concepts* that children make sense of their world:

> Thus a small child will have a concept of 'big things' … a concept of 'wetness' … a concept of 'things I like' and of 'things I don't like', and so on. When encountering novel objects or experiences, or faced with problems of any kind, a child attempts to make sense of them by fitting them into the range of concepts already held. If these concepts prove inadequate, he or she may have to modify them in some way, or perhaps try to develop a new concept altogether …

> (p52)

ASSIMILATION AND ACCOMMODATION

It is also important to understand two further key processes that lie at the heart of how Piaget believed children act upon their environments, namely *assimilation* and *accommodation*. It is through acting on their environments that children *assimilate* and then *accommodate* information that is new to them, and it is this process that guides their learning. *Assimilation* can be understood as new information that is absorbed by children into their *schemas* without any real manipulation of that information taking place. In contrast, *accommodation* is where relevant *schemas* then adapt in order that this new information can be stored.

PIAGET'S STAGES OF COGNITIVE DEVELOPMENT

Piaget believed that cognitive development in children follows a series of stages (Figure 3.1), proposing that these are 'invariant', meaning that children pass through one stage before progressing on to the next.

FOCUS ON THEORY

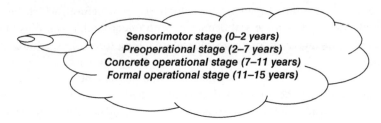

Sensorimotor stage (0–2 years)
Preoperational stage (2–7 years)
Concrete operational stage (7–11 years)
Formal operational stage (11–15 years)

Figure 3.1   Piaget's stages of cognitive development

During the *sensorimotor stage*, infants are learning through their senses (e.g. by sucking, touching and seeing the world around them). Piaget proposed that newly born infants are not capable of 'thinking', but rather engage in reflexive activities, such as grasping, that they have already been born with. As they develop, they will learn to sit, crawl, walk and use their first words, and then phrases and sentences, and so on.

During the *preoperational stage*, most children will be attending early years settings and will make the transition into primary school. Language is the key feature of this stage as this greatly extends their capacity to build *schemas* through *assimilation* and *accommodation*. This stage involves two further substages, *preconceptual* (2-4 years) and *intuitive* (4-7 years). In the former, children engage increasingly in imaginative and symbolic play using words and symbols to represent objects and individuals around them; imitation of the behaviours of others is frequent. Thinking during this stage may be limited by factors such as *egocentrism* and *rigidity of thinking* when, for example, children appear unable to view the world around them from the perspective of others (see example below). They may not have fully developed to an intellectual level, which allows them to reverse the order of sequences and adapt their thinking to account for changes in the appearance of their immediate environment. Thinking continues to be dominated by actual characteristics of objects, such as their shape, size and colour, as opposed to being guided by logic, which will come later. Children, for example, at this stage, who watch their teacher pouring a fixed amount of liquid from a short fat glass into a tall slim glass may continue to believe that there is now more water in the taller glass. Piaget referred to this type of thinking as *conservation*, and suggested that children's capacity to *conserve* marks the end of this stage and the beginning of the next.

EXAMPLE

Egocentrism and *rigidity of thinking*

Egocentrism attempts to explain young children's apparent inability to view the world from the perspective of others. Take the case of Zara, who at 2 years of age is playing the game of 'hide and seek' with her older brother. When she covers both her eyes, she thinks that her older brother is unable to see her. Piaget suggested that *egocentrism* pervades all of children's thinking at this age, and could, he believed, explain why young children ascribe feelings to objects around them.

With *rigidity of thinking*, Piaget believed that children at this age have not yet developed their thinking to a level where they can reverse sequences and adapt meaningfully and purposefully to changes in appearance. After I (the author) became a father for the first time, I recall being tasked with looking after my 2-year-old son while his mother went shopping for the day. I decided to make some lunch and cooked four sausages together with some beans and mashed potatoes. I then sat my son in his high chair with his little bowl. I put two sausages in his bowl and two on my plate. Because I was feeling particularly hungry and because I like sausages so much, I decided to take back one of my son's sausages for myself, giving me three sausages and leaving him with one. Big mistake! When he saw he had only one sausage, he went into spasms of anger, throwing his head back and screaming. Because I had studied Piaget during my psychology degree, I knew immediately what to do! I reached over and very quickly cut my son's one sausage up into lots of smaller pieces – he immediately stopped crying, smiled, and put one of the pieces of his sausage in his mouth. Being at a stage where his thinking was still 'rigid', the sight of many pieces of sausage meant to him that he now had lots more, even though there was still only one sausage in his bowl. At the time, I thought, thank goodness for Piaget.

During the *concrete operational stage*, children develop their capacity to apply logic as a means of problem-solving. Piaget argued that logic, which is characterised by operational rules, develops gradually as children acquire new and better skills, and can therefore increasingly organise these skills into more complex structures within their brains. In this way, thinking becomes much more flexible, though it may still be subject to the constraints of needing to have concrete objects present.

During the *formal operational stage*, cognitive development has become much more flexible, with children being able to deal more efficiently with symbolic problem-solving. Thinking is far more logical and children will increasingly test out ideas as opposed to taking them at face value; they are more objective and reflective in their thinking.

ACTIVITY

View the following YouTube video: *Piaget's Theory of Cognitive Development* (**www.youtube.com/watch?v=lhcgYgx7aAA**). Then make a list of the key points in Piaget's theory that you believe will help you in your future work as a teacher.

PIAGET IN THE CLASSROOM

Importantly, Piaget recognised the inconsistencies that teachers observe in children's development, referring to this as 'horizontal decalage', where some children will readily succeed with certain tasks while other children of the same age will not. This is not a matter of how 'intelligent' children are, but rather a reflection of maturation and experience in acting upon different environments.

Piaget initially proposed that teaching should be appropriate to the age of the child, though he later changed his views on this, accepting that children's thinking can develop at very different rates, with some children, for example, being capable of engaging in quite sophisticated and intellectually challenging learning even at a young age. This is an important point as during the 1960s and 1970s, much practice in UK primary schools had been influenced by Piaget's original view that children may not have developed their thinking to levels whereby their teachers should progress them on to tasks that would typically be given to older children. Children were often held back from progressing on to more complicated and challenging learning activities that they would have been capable of; their teachers had been led to believe that children's thinking would not have developed to a level that would allow them to deal competently with such new learning. An example of this was the *concept* of 'readiness' and the belief that instead of accelerating children's learning, they should be viewed as having to have attained certain stages of readiness before their teachers should progress them; this was often the case with children starting school who could already read very well.

An interesting aspect of Piaget's work was that he was not only interested in how children come to acquire correct answers to problems, but importantly why they achieve incorrect answers. He was also particularly interested in the strategies that children use when thinking; this is now a recognised feature of practice in primary schools today. Trainee teachers are now tasked with understanding children's misconceptions and why they repeat errors. They are also expected to inform themselves about the type of strategies children use and identify those that are inefficient and even erroneous to their learning and progress. Though Piaget's views gained much acceptance at the time, they have in more recent decades generated much debate and been criticised, especially by those who view the cognitive development of children across general populations as being typically uneven.

ARE STAGES OF DEVELOPMENT FIXED AND UNIDIRECTIONAL?

While Piaget believed that children's intellectual or cognitive development can be explained in terms of *schemas* and how children interact with their environments through developmental stages that are 'invariant', other theorists have taken a different view. One such theorist was Lev Vygotsky, who, unlike Piaget, did not view stages of development as fixed and unidirectional, but rather as progressive and incremental. Instead, he proposed that children can move backwards as well as forwards in their stages of development, depending on factors such as their maturity and the nature of the challenges they are asked to deal with. Gray and MacBlain (2015) have explained Vygotsky's *concept* of stages as follows:

1. *Primitive stage: Children under 2 years of age use vocal activity as a means of emotional expression and for social engagement ... behaviour becomes increasingly purposeful and goal-directed ... thought and language are separate ...*

2. *Practical intelligence: During this stage, the child's language uses syntactic (rules of speech) and logical forms. These forms of speech are linked to the child's practical problem-solving activities ...*

3. *External symbolic stage: Thinking aloud is common ... with language used to help with internal problem solving ... Thinking aloud enables the child to self-regulate and plan their activities ...*

4. *Internalization of symbolic tools: Between 7 and 8 years of age, children internalize thinking ... Problem solving continues to be guided by speech but the voice is internal ... This stage leads to greater cognitive independence, flexibility and freedom.*

(p97)

─ **ACTIVITY** ────────────────────

View the following YouTube video: *Schemas, Assimilation, and Accommodation* (**www.youtube. com/watch?v=BMc9TPwoVxQ**). Then make a list of *schemas* that you have observed in children.

WHAT SHOULD GUIDE TEACHING: ABILITY OR ATTAINMENT?

Too often, teachers in primary school fail to recognise the true levels of intellectual functioning in some of their pupils and make judgements about children's natural intelligence that are based solely on their attainments in literacy and numeracy. It has been the author's experience over many years working as an educational psychologist that too many children have been perceived by their teachers to be of limited intellectual ability when in fact they are simply developing at a different rate to their peers and taking more time to acquire literacy skills and understand mathematical *concepts*. Too often, I have found, for example, when assessing children with poor literacy and/or numeracy skills that they are in fact intellectually very able but have specific learning difficulties, such as dyslexia, which have failed to be recognised by their teachers (MacBlain et al., 2015). The following case study clearly illustrates this and demonstrates how one child of above-average intellectual ability has experienced failure throughout his primary years because he has not had appropriate assessment. His specific learning difficulties in working memory and processing were not identified, and so appropriate interventions were not put in place and only became recognised following assessment by an educational psychologist prior to transferring to secondary school.

─ **CASE STUDY 3.1** ────────────────────

Assessment of intellectual development and effective teaching

Alfie has just turned 11 years of age and is in his final year of primary school. His progress in reading and writing has been very slow and his parents became very concerned about his poor progress after he entered Key Stage 2. His teachers in Key Stage 1 constantly assured Alfie's parents not to worry as his 'reading and spelling will come along quite soon'. They also described Alfie as having 'poor concentration' and as being 'very easily distracted'. His parents have had Alfie recently assessed privately by an educational psychologist, who reported as follows:

Psychometric assessment (Table 1) indicates that Alfie is of above-average ability but with specific learning difficulties relating to his working memory and processing speed, which have clearly impacted on his reading and spelling and written skills as well as his skills with numerical operations.

(Continued)

41

(Continued)

Table 1   Wechsler Intelligence Scale for Children (WISC-IV UK)

Area of assessment	Index score	Centile
Verbal comprehension	121	92
Perceptual reasoning	125	95
Working memory	80	9
Processing speed	83	13

Two-thirds of children are considered to function within the average range of ability, which is represented between the 16th and 84th centiles, with the 16th centile lying at the lowest end of the average range and the 84th centile at the highest. The 85th centile upwards represents increasingly higher ability, with the 95th centile representing the top 1 per cent of ability. At the other end of the range, the 1st centile represents the lowest 1 per cent of ability.

The verbal comprehension index has been designed to offer a measure of verbal reasoning and concept formation. The perceptual reasoning index measures fluid reasoning within the perceptual domain with tasks that access such elements as non-verbal concept formation, organisation and visual perception, simultaneous processing, and visual motor coordination. Working memory is an individual's ability to attend to and hold information in short-term memory while performing operations or the manipulation of these, and then accurately producing the transformed information. Processing speed offers an indication of the speed with which simple or routine information can be processed while not making errors.

Assessment of Alfie's literacy skills are offered in Table 2.

Table 2   Literacy scores

Test	Standard score	Centile
Word recognition	82	12
Reading comprehension	91	27
Spelling	83	13

It is clear that Alfie is continuing to experience significant difficulties in most aspects of literacy. It appeared to me that Alfie finds much of the reading and spelling process to be confusing. I noted, for example, that when I invited him to name the vowels, he appeared very confused and responded with the following: 'd', 'u', 'a', 'e' and 'b'. Alfie was also unable to recite the whole alphabet in correct sequence. I believe that the severity and impact of Alfie's specific learning difficulties in working memory and processing speed are not well understood by his teachers, and I would suggest that these have in the past been misinterpreted as poor concentration and as Alfie being easily distracted and lacking motivation when asked to complete written tasks. It is my view that Alfie will benefit from the following:

- *Acquiring a much better understanding of the structural analysis of words, in particular how words are formed using roots, prefixes and suffixes.*

- *Having daily access to literacy programmes that are structured, sequential and cumulative and that incorporate a great deal of multisensory techniques. Such an approach will help enormously in compensating for his much weaker difficulties in working memory and processing speed.*

- *Regular reinforcement of new learning.*

- *Employing a cursive script of writing and being taught to sound out each letter as he writes it, and to then clearly speak the whole word he has just written.*

- *Alfie will also benefit enormously from being shown how to construct his own books, which should contain drawings and pictures that are familiar to him, and with each of these having a short meaningful phrase or sentence of no more than five words constructed from his own natural language - this is very important.*

- *Weekly opportunities to use digital technology to support word recognition, reading comprehension and spelling, and to provide him with additional opportunities to record and check written activities.*

- *Regular opportunities to demonstrate his high level of intellectual ability in front of his peers - this will work to develop his self-esteem and self-confidence.*

It is clear from the educational psychologist's assessment that despite being of 'above-average ability', Alfie has struggled with most aspects of literacy, which has prevented him from properly accessing the curriculum and being able to demonstrate his very high level of cognitive ability, which is well above average and higher than the majority of children of his age. It is also clear that much of his school-based learning has not been at a level that matches his true intellectual ability and his potential to achieve well in formal education, had his specific learning difficulties been recognised and appropriate interventions put in place to effectively manage these. Alfie is an example of a child whose development in some areas of intellectual functioning has not matched others, with the result that he has been viewed by his teachers as not being very able because of poor attainments in literacy and numeracy. Alfie is in fact 'brighter' than most of his class peers who don't have developmental difficulties with working memory and the speed at which their brains process certain types of information.

NEUROSCIENCE: NEW UNDERSTANDINGS IN CHILD DEVELOPMENT

It is astonishing how few books written on the subject of children's learning contain references to the brain, and yet it is this one organism that controls, regulates and drives children's learning. It is also astonishing that trainee teachers are not expected to understand the workings of the brain and how it develops and regulates intellectual functioning. To begin to understand brain development, we need to look initially at the role played by neurons, as it is through these that information in the brain passes in the form of electrical impulses.

THE STRUCTURE OF THE BRAIN

It is estimated that the number of neurons in the brain is in the region of many billions, and it is while the foetus is developing prior to birth that neurons are formed and then form different parts of the brain. As this process progresses, neurons also establish responses to chemicals in the brain, beginning with the more primitive areas of the brain, namely the brainstem, where autonomic functions required for bodily development lie. At the point of birth, these functions are relatively well developed, meaning that the infant has the capacity to breathe, sleep, hear and experience sensations, and be nourished by sucking for milk. In the days and weeks following birth, more advanced areas of the brain develop (e.g. the cerebral cortex, which is needed for higher-order functioning, such as cognitive, emotional and language development). It is during the early years that the majority of brain development occurs, and different areas of the brain develop their own functions, which also requires the use of chemical agents such as hormones and neurotransmitters.

SYNAPSES

In the first months and years of life, children learn at an accelerating pace, and this requires the strengthening of connections between neurons. Neurons do not connect directly with one another, but rather have tiny spaces or gaps between them, known as *synapses*, across which impulses travel. Hardy and Heyes (1994) have explained this as follows:

> All messages in the nervous system are carried in the form of nerve impulses, but their interpretation depends upon which part of the brain receives the message: in one part an impulse might be interpreted as a spot of light, in another as a sound … Many of the so-called 'nerve gases' produced for warfare work by preventing the destruction of the transmitter molecules; death results from the continual excitation of many neurons which causes prolonged contraction of all of the muscles of the body.
>
> (pp262–2)

Synapses develop at an extraordinary rate during early development; it is understood, for example, that the cerebral cortex in infants can develop more than a million synapses every second. Though many synapses become established, many do not and are lost to the child. While this process continues throughout life, by adolescence around half of the synapses will have been lost; it is recognised that brains work on the principle 'use it or lose it', as connections between neurons become lost if not used. In this manner, connections between neurons that are used a lot become more permanent and durable. As this process continues, children create and develop stronger pathways, which result in the brain becoming organised.

MYELINATION

The more children interact purposefully and meaningfully with their environments, the stronger the connections in the brain and the more secure their foundations for future learning; this is particularly the case with language. An additional feature of early brain development is *myelination*, where a fatty substance known as myelin acts as an insulator and permits the transmission of impulses across synapses. The stimulation experienced by infants and young children can affect the myelination process and future learning. By the time children attend preschool, their brains will have almost grown fully in size. An important aspect of brain development in young children is that they have the capacity to adapt to their environments; young children need stimulation and enriching experiences. Children also need to be loved and cared for as it is through love and care that they develop those parts of their brain that extend their capacity to live emotionally fulfilled lives.

FACTORS AFFECTING BRAIN DEVELOPMENT

The importance of the genetic make-up inherited by children and the experiences they have in their environments is now far better understood than ever before. We know that the quality of the relationships between young children and their primary caregivers is an important element in early brain development. We also know that the more young children engage in movement and language, the stronger the connections in their brains. Early experiences are very important for future development and learning. A preschool child who, for example, is read to each night before going to sleep in a loving way will form connections in his brain that will be different to those of a child whose parents allow him to stay up watching television and typically communicate with him in monosyllabic terms and by shouting. If the first child is also given many opportunities to engage in creative play and physical exercise, he will also develop stronger sensorimotor connections than the latter child, who will be spending too much time sitting and passively watching television. In addition, the first child, whose parents employ rich and varied vocabulary when talking with him and explaining things, will also develop stronger and qualitatively better semantic networks than the latter child, whose parents offer little in the way of vocabulary development.

NEUROSCIENCE AND EDUCATION

Recently, Hohnen and Murphy (2016, p75) drew attention to how attempts are being made across the globe to integrate emerging research in neuroscience into how we seek to understand and explain children's learning, though they also emphasised how, in doing so, 'there continues to be a debate in the field about how fruitful a relationship this might be' (Ansari et al., 2011). Despite this ongoing debate regarding the fruitfulness of the relationship, it is nonetheless necessary to recognise that neuroscience has much to offer trainee teachers who wish to gain a better and much deeper understanding of how children's emotional, social, physical and cognitive development impact on their learning (Whitebread and Sinclair-Harding, 2014). With advances in our knowledge of the structure and functioning of the brain, we are now beginning to better understand how the developing brain in young children interfaces with the types of environments they are born into, and subsequently grow and mature. Acknowledging the importance of the genetic make-up inherited by children and the life experiences they have in their early environments can offer trainee teachers many insights into how children learn and what factors promote learning or act as a hindrance to it.

Some years ago, Howard-Jones (2014) undertook a review into the relationship between neuroscience and education, in collaboration with the Wellcome Trust, which examined 'the extent to which insights from the sciences of mind and brain influence, or are close to influencing, classroom practice' (p2). The review gathered information from teachers and parents, as well as students, and also undertook an exploration of the neuroscience literature. The review summarised education evidence regarding approaches and interventions that were claimed to be based on evidence from the field of neuroscience. The review was structured around 18 topics, each of which was considered against the evidence of its educational effectiveness and the 'distance that needs to be travelled for the neuroscience knowledge to be applied within the classroom'. It also offered insights into how neuroscience has informed education as well as how neuroscience can be used to inform future practice in education. Howard-Jones (2014) stressed how:

Anything that has an impact on learning will ultimately have a brain basis; the idea that our understanding about how the brain works could impact upon educational practice is therefore an attractive one.

(p3)

In his review, Howard-Jones (2014) also indicated how neuroscience has the potential to offer a great deal to education (e.g. in relation to how children think when completing mathematical activities):

Maths anxiety interferes with neurocognitive processes crucial to learning … Cognitive neuroscience has made a substantial contribution to understanding how numerical abilities develop in young children and the foundational role of non-symbolic and symbolic representation in acquiring formal mathematical skills. We now understand that quantitative ability involves a number of components, and these include:

- *a non-symbolic number system (or numerosity) which is the ability to quickly understand and approximate numerical quantities … considered to be evident … very early in human development.*

- *a symbolic number system which is the ability to understand representations such as '3' or 'three', whose development is strongly linked to that of early language, beginning around 2–3 years old.*

- *ability to map between non-symbolic and symbolic systems, which appears linked to the use of fingers and develops through early childhood.*

(p13)

It is clear from Howard-Jones' review that neuroscience has much to offer teachers. It is now accepted that neuroscience is informing our understanding of children's cognitive, emotional and social development, as well as learning (Kokkinaki and Vasdekis, 2015; Whitebread, 2012).

CHAPTER SUMMARY

- Trainee teachers need to understand what cognitive development in young children looks like.

- They also need to have knowledge of and understand different theoretical approaches that explain children's thinking and learning, which should inform their practice.

- Trainee teachers should understand the importance of differentiating between ability and attainment and basing their teaching on accurate assessments of children's potential, and not just on their attainments in literacy and numeracy.

- All teachers should know how language shapes development and learning in each individual child.

- Trainee teachers should acknowledge the contribution that neuroscience is making to our understanding of children's learning.

- Schools should strive to ensure a healthy balance between delivering target-driven curricula and allowing teachers time to observe and assess how different levels of cognitive development affect their pupils' learning outcomes.

EXTENDED READING

Gray, C. and MacBlain, S.F. (2015) *Learning Theories in Childhood* (2nd edn). London: SAGE. This text examines in detail the ideas of Jean Piaget alongside other theorists; it is very readable and highly relevant to trainee teachers preparing to work in primary schools.

Hohnen, B. and Murphy, T. (2016) 'The optimum context for learning: drawing on neuroscience to inform best practice in the classroom', *Educational & Child Psychology*, 33(1): 75–90. This is a very interesting and relevant article that addresses key aspects of neuroscience and how these can inform best practice in the classroom; importantly, the article addresses the importance of context in children's learning within an excellent journal.

4

CHILDREN'S SOCIAL DEVELOPMENT

WHY YOU SHOULD READ THIS CHAPTER

Our understanding of how social factors impact on children's development and learning has only in recent decades come to be properly researched. While teachers and policymakers in previous decades were aware that adverse social factors could have negative consequences for children's development, it is only in recent years that they have begun to properly acknowledge their impact. The emergence of recent social drivers, such as materialism, a growing drug culture and an unprecedented expansion of social media, has added to the challenges facing researchers, academics and practitioners seeking to better understand how children's social development impacts on their learning.

By the end of this chapter, you should know:

- what characterises social development;

- how children's moral development impacts on their social and academic learning;

- how environmental factors, such as the family and poverty, shape children's development and learning;

- the importance of developing strong self-efficacy in children;

- how social fears can impact on children's development and learning; and

- the importance of teachers supporting children's social development and how this underpins the standards required for UK Qualified Teaching Status (QTS).

INTRODUCTION

From birth, children engage in an increasing variety of ways with others and with the world around them, and in doing so grow to be social beings capable of relating purposefully with others and understanding the rules and conventions that define the communities, societies and cultures they are born into. It is fundamental, therefore, that trainee teachers properly recognise and understand how children's social development is intertwined with their cognitive, physical and emotional development, and how this complex and ever-shifting interplay of factors impacts on the dynamics of children's learning. The part that social development plays in children's overall development and learning is evidenced within the standards for Qualified Teaching Status (QTS) in the UK. While all of the standards link in some way to children's social development, the following are used as a focus for this chapter.

WHAT DOES SOCIAL DEVELOPMENT LOOK LIKE?

The nature of social development in children is highly complex and is perhaps best understood as an accumulation of factors, many of which are hidden and some of which have far greater importance than others for their learning. Let us look, for example, at how physical growth influences children's social development. We know, of course, that as children grow, they change physically in height and appearance; we also know that they progress at different rates in their acquisition of skills and abilities to engage with other children and adults through physical activities, such as running, jumping, climbing and playing games such as 'hide and seek'. As their physical skills and abilities develop, children can increasingly socialise with their peers in new and different ways; in doing so, they gain self-confidence, build self-esteem and enhance their self-efficacy, all of which are essential building blocks for future relationships and all of which go to form their own unique identities as individuals.

▬ KEY THEORY ▬

Understanding the complex nature of social development in young children

The complexity of social development in children has been well explained by Mercer (2018), who saw it as:

> *A series of changes by which children move from egocentric, self-centred, weakly empathic characteristics of early childhood, when they are unfamiliar with many conventions of social behaviour, to more adult-like characteristics that facilitate empathy, social interactions, relationships with adults and other children, and compliance with conventional standards of behaviour.*

(p166)

(Continued)

(Continued)

Importantly, Mercer recognises how social development involves not only change in *age*, but *experience*. Key Stage 1 teachers will, for example, observe the transitions of their pupils as they move through Key Stage 2 and into secondary school, and observe how many aspects of later development will have been formed during their first years of schooling. Interestingly, Mercer employs the descriptors, *'egocentric'*, *'self-centred'* and *'weakly empathic'* as key characteristics in children's social development. These descriptors should not just be viewed in a negative sense; instead, they should be understood within the context of children's wider cognitive development. It must be understood that there will be some children whose thinking and reasoning abilities might not as yet have matured sufficiently to understand the consequences of their actions. Equally, some children will not have acquired sufficient levels of language that allow them to express themselves adequately. Looking elsewhere in the literature, we find that Fontana (1995) chose to explain *egocentrism* in children in terms of an inability to 'see the world from anything other than a self-centred, subjective viewpoint' (p55).

Mercer's further reference to 'weakly empathic' characteristics in young children is especially relevant to how trainee teachers are now tasked with learning how to support and even manage the social development of children. While empathy cannot be directly taught and develops more fully in some children than others, there is, however, a great deal that teachers can do to progress this aspect of children's functioning. Referring to the place of activities employed by teachers to develop empathy, such as role-playing in drama sessions and using 'simple imaginative descriptions' of the nature of emotions experienced by others, Fontana (1995) offered the following:

> Unless prompted by such activities, some children even at the stage of formal operations seem never to have considered what it must be like to be at the butt of class teasing, or to be old and unwanted, or to grow up against a background of family violence.

> (p247)

Mercer also identifies 'compliance with conventional standards of behaviour' as a key feature in social development. Here, trainee teachers should reflect upon the importance of creating and then managing classroom and school environments that promote compliance; they should also reflect on how they might directly and indirectly intervene to ensure that pupils learn to comply with conventional standards of behaviour. For the majority of pupils, this will occur almost automatically, but for a minority the picture may be different; not all children entering Key Stage 1 will have embarked upon a positive path of learning how to comply with standards outside of their homes. Some children will, for example, have internalised as normal behaviour patterns that have been modelled to them by dysfunctional parents, not to mention antisocial behaviours they might have observed in their local communities from other irresponsible children and teenagers.

RELATING TO OTHERS

As children enter Key Stage 1, they should be capable of demonstrating understanding of many of their own feelings in relation to those of their peers and adults, and will typically have the capacity to comfort others, such as a friend who is upset and crying. As they move through Key Stage 1, they will be able to describe more complex feelings they observe in others. Cowie (2012) has explained this as follows:

By 8 or 9 years of age, children ... can speculate about how another person might feel; for example, a child might be feeling unappreciated because they have low self-esteem even though they played well in a team.

(p17)

During their school placements, trainee teachers working with children across Key Stages 1 and 2 will quickly become aware of differences in the social development of pupils and how, for example, children of different ages perceive and respond to the emotions and feelings of their peers, as well as those adults they come into contact with. Importantly, they may find that in Key Stage 2, some pupils present as being socially very immature, as might be evidenced in how they fail to understand the emotions of others and behave in ways that are more characteristic of much younger children. This may be due to early experiences in their families where parents have been poor role models who are emotionally detached and who model inconsistent and even aggressive responses to them and to each other. It is important, therefore, that trainee teachers recognise the need to support these pupils in reflecting on how others around them experience and manage emotions in different ways, and how to apply what they learn from observing others to managing their own feelings and behaviours; in this way, children come to learn about themselves and develop sensitivity to others, both of which underpin empathic thinking and positive social development.

MORAL DEVELOPMENT

A key aspect of children's social development is their sense of morality and what they believe to be right and wrong, which affects how they perceive the actions of others and how they come to understand their own actions. A notable figure in this field is Kohlberg (1981), who extended the original ideas of Piaget to propose six stages of moral development. Fontana (1995) has encapsulated the first four stages, which are especially relevant to teachers in the primary years, as follows:

Preconventional morality (Piaget's preoperational stage of thinking) ... 2–7 years

1. *Punishment and obedience. Children have no real moral sense ... behaviour can be shaped by simple reinforcement.*

2. *Individualism, instrumental purpose, and exchange. A 'right' action is one that works for the child personally. The child may appear able to meet the needs of others, but this is only because the result is directly favourable.*

Conventional morality (Piaget's concrete operational stage of thinking) ... 7–11 years

1. *Mutual interpersonal expectations, relationships, and interpersonal conformity. Children try to live up to the expectations of their elders, initially only in specific situations, but later more generally as they come to acquire a concept of the 'good' child.*

(Continued)

(Continued)

2. *Social system and conscience (law and order). Moral ideas generalize even further, and children try to live up to them not simply for personal gain, but because they now develop a sense of duty towards authority and the maintenance of the existing social order.*

(p239)

Fontana made the important point that for children to acquire a particular level of moral development, they must also be able to apply the appropriate level of thinking in situations that requires them to also behave appropriately; he saw this as a prerequisite for being at the corresponding level of moral development. The implications for teachers, therefore, are many. Some children in Key Stage 2 may not, for example, have reached an appropriate level of thinking and cognitive development to properly understand that their actions are unacceptable and misplaced, and might even be hurtful to others, despite being told repeatedly by their teachers that such actions are unacceptable and wrong. The continuing influence of families on the course of children's moral development throughout their primary years is, of course, very strong, and there may also be cultural differences and influences from children's communities that militate against them moving through the stages of moral development.

HOW ENVIRONMENT SHAPES DEVELOPMENT AND LEARNING

While all children are born with unique biological differences that shape social development, they are also influenced by the environments they are born into. Children from deprived inner-city environments will, for example, have different life experiences to those in rural affluent villages. Equally, children from affluent families where parents devote time to their children's needs may have different experiences to those from a one-parent family where the parent devotes time to their children but is constantly unemployed and struggling financially. Cultural beliefs also play a part in shaping children's lives, a factor that has become increasingly evident in the UK with the increase in 'new arrivals' from different parts of the world.

ACTIVITY

Reflect on those factors that impacted positively on your own early development. Then prioritise these from the most important to the least. Discuss with others how your community might have influenced these.

FAMILIES AND THEIR IMPORTANCE FOR SOCIAL DEVELOPMENT

Children typically gain their first social experiences in families, and from birth observe the behaviour patterns of those around them, most often parents and older siblings. These will be the first social relationships they form, and the nature of these relationships will impact on them for the rest of their lives. This said, families are changing!

SEPARATION AND DIVORCE

The nature of families has in recent decades changed significantly, with a growing number of children now being born outside of marriage, an increase in cohabitation, and high levels of separation and divorce, with subsequent re-partnering, which also often leads to the birth of other children. Many professionals and academics now prefer to use the term 'household' as opposed to 'family'. In some instances, newly formed stepfamilies may try to reduce children's recognition of their previous family (Castrén and Widmer, 2015), which then results in the children having less contact with previous family members, such as aunts and uncles and grandparents; this can have a detrimental impact on some children's sense of security and even limit important life experiences. All of these factors will, to some extent, impact upon children's social development and even their learning; while the impact may be detrimental to some children, there may be other cases where there are positive outcomes for a child, such as when a mother leaves an abusive relationship and forms a new family structure, which offers her children stability, consistency and safety.

Unforeseen financial hardships following separation and/or divorce can also be an important factor in children's social development and even have adverse effects on their learning. Separation and divorce can also mean for some children that they live between two households where expectations and experiences are very different. A recent study undertaken by Sadowski and McIntosh (2016) found that some children reported having a sense of longing for their absent parent, which then impacted on how they adjusted to new parenting arrangements. In more extreme cases, Sadowski and McIntosh found that shared time between both parents could even result in children feeling they had two 'absent' parents, leaving them in a constant state of longing. Importantly, a previous study undertaken by Sarkadi et al. (2008) found that involvement by fathers in the lives of their children reduced psychological problems in girls and behavioural problems in boys. Other research (Ross et al., 2012) has shown how many very young fathers come from low socio-economic backgrounds, are less-well educated, have fewer employment prospects and might have a background involving delinquent behaviour.

HAVE GRANDPARENTS A ROLE TO PLAY IN CHILDREN'S SOCIAL DEVELOPMENT?

It is estimated (Gautier et al., 2013) that between 200,000 and 300,000 children in the UK are being reared by grandparents because of such problems as the death of a parent, drug or alcohol abuse, and imprisonment. Grandparents typically act as mentors and offer nurture to their grandchildren. They are also able to intervene at times of family crises and may offer support during times of family breakdown; in many instances, they can fill gaps in the parenting of children, which may alleviate potential problems in their social development.

LGBT FAMILIES

Families where children are raised by LGBT parents are becoming more common; in part, this is because of recent changes in legislation. The Civil Partnership Act came into effect in the UK in 2005, and this allowed same-sex couples to form civil partnerships, according them much greater rights and greater recognition in society; the Marriage (Same Sex Couples) Act 2013 in the UK allowed the first same-sex marriages to take place in England and Wales in March 2014. Scotland followed, with the first same-sex marriages taking place in December 2014. Though civil partnerships are legal within Northern Ireland, no legislation has been passed for same-sex marriage despite a recent survey indicating that the majority of a survey sample (58 per cent) were in favour of it (ARK, 2014). Same-sex couples now have the right to adopt children following the introduction of the Adoption and Children Act 2002 in England and Wales and the Adoption and Children (Scotland) Act 2007. In 2014, it was estimated that there were some 84,000 families consisting of same-sex parents, with 11 per cent of these families having dependent children (ONS, 2015). The UK government reported in 2015 that the number of children adopted by gay and lesbian families was at a record high, with 480 children having been placed in such a family during the 12 months between March 2014 and March 2015 (GOV.UK, 2015). The Equality Act 2010 makes it illegal in England, Scotland and Wales to discriminate against anyone because of their sexual orientation. It is now recognised that there is a need for training programmes for teachers that will enable them to feel more comfortable and more prepared in their work with these families (Hegde et al., 2014). Some have even suggested that teachers need to unlearn stereotypes and biases in a move towards greater inclusivity in how they teach (Kintner-Duffy et al., 2012).

POVERTY

One very clear way in which environment impacts on children's social development and on their learning is poverty. Only a decade ago, Cullis and Hansen (2009) drew attention to the impact of low incomes on the learning of children in the UK when they indicated how every £100 of extra income in the first nine months of children's lives leads to a difference of around a month's development by the age of 5 years, when children commence their formal schooling (p13). A year later, Field (2010) described how:

> Children from low income families in the UK often grow up to be poor adults ... [they] are more likely to have preschool conduct and behavioural problems; more likely to experience bullying and take part in risky behaviours as teenagers; less likely to do well at school; less likely to stay on at school after 16; and more likely to grow up to be poor themselves.

(p28)

Many children growing up in the 'poorest' families frequently fail to have access to good reading material in their homes, limited learning activities and limited access to computers, all of which can be detrimental to their progress at school. In a report entitled *Deprivation and Risk: The Case for Early Intervention* (Action for Children, 2010), Dr Ruth Lupton captured the impact of poverty on many young children in the UK today when she stressed:

> The relationship between deprivation and educational attainment is striking. Across the UK, children from the poorest homes start school with more limited vocabularies and greater likelihood of conduct problems and hyperactivity ... During primary school UK children fall further behind, and even the brightest children from the most disadvantaged backgrounds are overtaken by the age of 10 by their better-off peers who start off behind them.

(p12)

More recently, in his annual report, *Unsure Start: HMCI's Early Years Annual Report 2012/13 Speech 2014*, Sir Michael Wilshaw, Her Majesty's Chief Inspector (Ofsted), stressed how poverty and low income, particularly in the early years, can have a detrimental impact upon children's learning, and ultimately their life choices (Wilshaw, 2014). In terms of social development, Wilshaw stressed how children from the poorest backgrounds, 'are less likely to follow instructions, make themselves understood, manage their own basic hygiene or play well together'. Wilshaw went on to emphasise that 'By age five, many children have started reading simple words, talking in sentences and can add single numbers. But far fewer of the poorest can do these things well'. Very worryingly, he also drew attention to how those children who grew up in low-income families are 'far more likely than their better-off peers to lag behind at age three ... Too many do badly by the end of primary, and carry on doing badly' (p3). A further and very worrying aspect of poverty, as indicated by Wilshaw, was the degree to which children from the poorest families who are intellectually very able can fail to gain access to high-achieving and academically inspiring schools where they might have greater opportunities to demonstrate their natural intelligence and realise their potential. To further our understanding of the impact of poverty on children and how wider economic factors affect children and their families, it is worth looking at the work of the French sociologist and philosopher Pierre Bourdieu, who has added a great deal to our understanding of the complex nature of societies and, perhaps more particularly, the impact of 'class' on children's development, and therefore their learning.

▬ KEY THEORY ▬

The importance of cultural capital in children's development

Bourdieu has led many to question aspects of modern society, and more specifically institutionalised structures, and how these impact upon children's development and learning. Bourdieu has suggested that cultures found among the 'upper' classes are typically superior to those in the 'lower' classes. Individuals in the former, he suggests, typically assert that lack of progress and failure in children is due to the individuals themselves. He proposed that when failure among children in the lower classes is measured through lack of success in examinations, this is erroneous because, he asserts, failure needs to be understood as a direct consequence of education systems, and not because of the cultures in which children grow and learn. Readers may wish to consider the degree to which education has been shaped by independent or 'private, fee-paying' schools and the benefits that children attending such schools have gained over those children who have not. Bourdieu has argued that education systems reproduce the cultural values of the upper classes who have historically dominated societies; by imposing these values, they have come to be accepted by most people and even legitimised, with the result that the culture of the upper classes has become viewed as desirable by the lower classes. Bourdieu viewed this possession of values by the upper classes in terms of 'cultural capital'. Children born into the upper-class cultures have, he argued, an inherent advantage over children who are not, in that they are socialised into what is perceived to be the ideal and desired culture by all. This, in turn, affects their attainment in formal education systems. Bourdieu has also talked of a *concept, habitus,* that refers largely to lifestyle, expectations held by individuals, their actions and behaviours, and so on. The *habitus* of different classes, he argues, is different, and therefore results in different expectations, aspirations and thinking that informs decision-making. The actions and behaviours, expectations and aspirations observed by children

(Continued)

(Continued)

within their *habitus* influence not only their own behaviours, but very importantly their internal representations of how they themselves think they can interact with others in society and how they can develop their own abilities and skills, their talents and their potential. Bourdieu viewed formal education as being a means by which children become marginalised; readers may wish to reflect on how some children growing up in economically deprived areas may become marginalised from more 'well-off' children, who often follow a well-defined path where they are expected to and supported in achieving highly at school and going on to study at university before commencing professional careers.

When seeking to understand how social development impacts on children and their learning, it is also useful to consider how children themselves act upon their own development. One very fruitful area of study is to be found in the work of Albert Bandura and his ideas on 'self-efficacy'.

SELF-EFFICACY

Bandura (1977a) promoted the idea of 'self-efficacy', which he saw as children's belief in their ability to succeed with different tasks and in different situations, and importantly the capacity they have acquired to exercise control over their actions. He suggested that self-efficacy is closely related to how children think, their actions and their emotional state.

RECOGNISING POOR SELF-EFFICACY IN CHILDREN

Children with poor self-efficacy may be observed to avoid tasks that present them with a significant challenge, preferring to focus their thinking on negative thoughts. If trainee teachers look carefully when on school placements, they may observe some pupils presenting with characteristics of self-efficacy. These children will typically demonstrate poor self-confidence and low self-esteem, and generally underperform in comparison to those with high levels of self-efficacy. They may, for example, be much more reluctant to attempt new tasks and see these through to completion. They may display marked signs of anxiety, especially when asked by their teachers to solve problem-based learning tasks that present them with a challenge. Colverd and Hodgkin (2011) have suggested that such children often place limitations on what they think they are capable of and internalise belief systems whereby they believe that many problem-based tasks are beyond their ability when, in fact, this is not the case (p36).

Children with poor self-efficacy who are being asked by their teacher to work with other children for the first time on completing a mathematical problem may, for example, begin by saying to the other children, 'I don't want to do this', because they believe, incorrectly, that the problem will be beyond their ability. Such behaviours may, over time, result in the other pupils preferring not to work with them and even referring to them, among each other, as being 'stupid'. Having a lack of belief in one's own abilities can, over time, also adversely affect a child's motivation and eventually their commitment to learning. Bandura argued that a key element in children acquiring high levels of self-efficacy is their development of what he referred to as 'mastery' through experiences. He believed, for example, that children can do this by observing other children who are successful, being given positive affirmation from adults and peers when they are successful with particular tasks, and learning to recognise, understand and importantly regulate their own emotions.

▬ CASE STUDY 4.1

A trainee teacher works to develop self-efficacy in a pupil

Sophie is a trainee teacher on placement in a primary school in a socially disadvantaged area. In her observations of the class, she identifies two children who regularly withdraw when asked to attempt new tasks by their teacher. She observes how they shy away from some tasks without even attempting them and show strong tendencies to stick with tasks that are familiar to them. At the end of her first week, Sophie meets with the class teacher and they devise a structured activity for these two children for the next day, which will allow Sophie to observe their behaviours more closely. On the following day, Sophie takes the two children aside and presents them with the structured activity, which requires them to engage in a problem-solving task. Sophie begins by modelling a strategy to both children that results in successful completion of the task; she then encourages them to have a go. As both children begin to work on the activity, Sophie praises their attempts, and also indicates clearly to them at each stage those aspects of their attempts that are proving successful. When they have completed the task successfully, she then sits with them and explains carefully what they have done to be successful. She repeats this process twice per week, and after some weeks she starts to observe how both children are becoming more confident in attempting each new activity, and importantly their growing enthusiasm for joining in with peers, even suggesting to their peers how some tasks should be approached.

▬ KEY THEORY

Bandura's relevance today

The theorist Albert Bandura challenged many of the popular notions of children's development of his time, and his ideas remain highly relevant even today. Bandura is perhaps best known for his 'social learning theory' (Bandura, 1977b), the name of which he changed to 'social cognitive theory' in 1986 in order to emphasise the highly complex nature of children's thinking and how they learned. He viewed social factors as being immensely important in helping us understand how children learn, and argued that children's learning did not always result in changes in behaviour on the basis that a child might spend time observing others without these observations (*stimuli*) resulting in changes in their own behaviour (*response*). He further argued that motivation is central to children's learning and that a child's level of motivation can influence how they observe the behaviours of others; in this way, their motivation contributes to their learning. Bandura proposed two further key factors in children's learning, *imitation* and *identification*.

(Continued)

(Continued)

Imitation and identification

Bandura suggested that children imitate the actions of and identify with those around them; in doing so, they *assimilate* new learning into *concepts* that they have already internalised and that structure their thinking. It is through such a process that new patterns of behaviour come to be memorised within children's thinking, which then enables them to act in ways they believe adults would act; it is important, therefore, that the behaviours being modelled by adults are appropriate. Bandura also noted how symbolic modelling, which is when children imitate and identify with fictional characters such as those found in stories and on television, is an important source of imitation for children. Bandura proposed that children not only observe the physical behaviours of those around them, but also verbal behaviours and the expectations they observe others making of them (Linden, 2005). Children, he argued, observe adults as they communicate verbal narratives to one another and seek to describe events that have taken place in their own lives or elsewhere; in doing so, the adults not only use spoken language, but also employ movements and gestures to convey what they are relating or describing, as well as conveying their own personal interpretations of events. Bandura further suggested the existence of a form of symbolic modelling where teachers, for example, can observe their pupils engaging in imitation and identifying with fictional characters they read about or watch on television and, more recently, computer simulations.

— CASE STUDY 4.2

Implementing strategies for developing self-efficacy

Ms Jones has just taken up her first teaching position as a Key Stage 1 teacher. A new child named Alex has moved to the area and has just joined her class. Previous reports written by Alex's play-group manager have emphasised that he 'is a very shy little boy who experiences difficulty with forming and maintaining friendships with other children'. Ms Jones observes Alex to be lacking in confidence, and though he is still very young she also notes that he has low self-efficacy, characterised by his unwillingness to attempt new tasks and saying to her that he doesn't want to try new tasks. Ms Jones decides on a course of action to start improving Alex's self-efficacy, and begins by arranging a number of activities when Alex can work alongside two other children, Tony and Sasha, both of whom are very confident children. She observes over the coming days and weeks how Alex starts to imitate Tony and Sasha in their behaviours and starts to use some of the same vocabulary and phrases they use. She also observes how Tony and Sasha take time to support Alex and to demonstrate to him how to do those parts of the activity they find easy but that he struggles with. After only a few months, Ms Jones notes how Alex's confidence has increased, as characterised by a growing belief he appears to have in his willingness to attempt new tasks by himself. She also notes that Alex's language is improving significantly and that he has adopted some of Tony and Sasha's behaviour patterns, most particularly their willingness to offer suggestions when problem-solving with the other children. Towards the end of the academic year, Ms Jones meets with Alex's next teacher in Key Stage 2 and explains the strategy she has used. Alex's next teacher continues to implement the strategy throughout his first year in Key Stage 2 and is very heartened by Alex's growth in self-confidence and his growing belief in what he feels he can achieve.

SOCIAL FEARS: THEIR IMPACT ON DEVELOPMENT

All children experience anxiety and social fears in some form during their lives, often emanating from aspects of the environments in which they grow up and events that they witness or are made aware of by significant others.

ACTIVITY

Reflect on those factors that made you fearful as a child and discuss with others how these factors might have affected your learning while at school. How did you manage these fears?

What makes one child experience anxiety and fear in their immediate environment or events in their lives might motivate and even excite another child. Much, of course, depends upon the nature of the environmental factors and the events, but much also depends upon the social maturity of the child, their emotional state at the time and their previous life experiences. While the question of how children experience anxiety and social fears is not fully understood, it is nevertheless generally agreed that the way in which children experience anxiety and social fears changes as they develop. Some children may experience social anxiety when they are fearful of situations where they have to interact with others or when they become the focus of others' attention. Here, it is worth trainee teachers considering how children new to a class may be fearful of talking with other children or speaking out in class.

SOCIALLY INDUCED ANXIETY

Children worry about what others might think of them, and especially if they think their peers and adults think badly of them or if they have done something that they think will be seen by their peers as silly. Such worries may be found in children as young as 4 years of age and typically result in behaviours such as blushing; however, where a child has internalised their feelings in an exaggerated form, they may experience higher levels of anxiety, leading to more acute responses such as trembling and even nausea. Children with social anxieties may be extremely shy and may experience significant difficulties when meeting other children for the first time or when asked to work with classmates in group activities. They may have few friends and belong to few friendship groups and may be observed by their teachers to avoid social situations because they feel they will be the centre of attention. Often these behaviours are more noticeable during unstructured time in school when, for example, children are left to play and interact with their peers without adults being present. All too frequently, poor interactions with other children go unnoticed by teachers unless, of course, the children are causing problems in the playground. While shyness is not a significant problem for the majority of children in primary schools and can be considered to be relatively normal, it becomes problematic when this aspect of a child's development leads to a lack of social engagement with others, thereby interfering with emotional well-being.

GENDER

The issue of gender has in recent years received a great deal of public attention. Knowles (2013), cited in Knowles and Holmström (2013), outlined a number of complexities that are central to the issue of gender as follows:

> At birth, usually depending on primary sex characteristics, children are normally determined as being boys or girls, male or female. However, although male and female can be termed biological distinctions, many argue that we have control over how we manifest our gender, particularly in terms of our behaviours, attitudes, values and beliefs. When identifying our gender we may say we are male, female or transgender, and there is considerable argument over whether the way we manifest that gender is genetic or learnt behaviour.

(p37)

Drawing a reference to the earlier work of Fausto-Sterling (2000), Knowles and Holmström (2013) indicated how:

> not only are there instances where there is ambiguity about the primary sex characteristics that are present at birth, where 'scientists, medical professionals, and the wider public have made sense of (or ought to make sense of) bodies that present themselves as neither entirely male nor female' (Fausto-Sterling, 2000, p3), but also there is more to being male or female than the physical characteristics of the body. That is to say: 'labeling someone a man or a woman is a social decision'.

(p37)

The issue of transgenderism affects children across the globe. In 2011, the UK government released a report, *Advancing Transgender Equality: A Plan for Action* (GOV.UK, 2011), setting out their commitment to tackling issues relating to transgenderism in the lives of young children, emphasising how prejudice and discrimination can not only scar the lives of individuals, but also 'undermine the principles upon which this country prides itself' (p6). The government of the day also emphasised how they were 'committed to making transgender equality a reality' (p5). The report further emphasised how it was necessary to tackle bullying while at the same time acknowledging that though some progress had been made, there was still much to do:

> Whilst the experiences of transgender pupils are least likely to be reflected in data and research ... we know that over 70 per cent of boys and girls who express gender variant behaviours are subject to bullying in schools ...

(p6)

The report also emphasised that tackling transphobic bullying is a crucial element in addressing behaviour that is unacceptable, therefore ensuring that society becomes more tolerant:

> This Government is committed to tackling transphobic bullying and we want to support schools to act as leaders and advocates for change. We have already issued anti-bullying guidance to support head teachers ... including transphobic bullying ... We are also issuing separate statutory guidance to extend head teachers' powers to respond to pupils who bully other pupils outside the school premises, and are reforming Ofsted schools' inspections to give all forms of prejudice-based bullying more prominence. But there is still a long way to go.

(p5)

DEVELOPMENT ACROSS EDUCATIONAL SETTINGS

Most, if not all, teachers will recall the time when they themselves started nursery school or playgroup and then moved to primary school. For most, the memories will be joyful, though for some these may be painful. Less than a decade ago, Choi (2012) emphasised how government departments in the UK had consistently drawn attention to an urgent need to target the transition between primary and secondary school, emphasising that this is a key factor in improving the attendance of many pupils (p29).

MOVING BETWEEN SETTINGS

Transitions from one setting to another are best understood in terms of a process that children undertake rather than events in their lives, and trainee teachers will need to appreciate that as Key Stage 1 teachers, they will play an active role in this process. Bronfenbrenner (1979, p26), cited in Kennedy et al. (2012), has explained transitions as when 'a person's position in the ecological environment is altered as a result of change in role, setting or both' (p20). This explanation is helpful as it gives particular emphasis to the changing 'role' of children that occurs when they transition from home, where they have an already established place, to the more formalised settings of playgroup and then school, which are populated by others who initially will be strangers to them. In these new environments, expectations of them will be different.

PREPARING FOR TRANSITION TO PRIMARY SCHOOL

Children are typically within their families when making the transition into more formalised educational settings and families will continue to exert significant influence over them. It is within their families that children first develop a capacity to manage new situations, which, of course, will vary greatly from one family to another. Each child's transition, however, from family to new and more formalised learning environments will be different; importantly, the actual process they go through when making these early transitions will be just as important as the outcomes (Crafter and Maunder, 2012). Here, it is worth emphasising how the theorist Bronfenbrenner viewed transitions in terms of a *dynamic process* that takes place between the child and the *social, historical* and *cultural* contexts they grow up in. All children grow up and develop in different social, historical and cultural contexts, of which schools are an integral part. Every primary school is unique and will, for example, have developed its own social, historical and cultural identity over many years, making them very different places for children entering into them. Importantly, Bronfenbrenner also believed transitions to be characterised by their reciprocity, in that the individual attributes children bring with them will affect the nature of the transitional process they undertake.

SOME IMPORTANT CONSIDERATIONS FOR TRAINEE TEACHERS

The way in which children experience transitions from one setting to another can have a huge impact on their social development and can in some cases greatly influence their learning. Trainee teachers should take time to assess and critically reflect on how informed they feel their own understanding is of the potential impact that moving from one setting to another will have on children, their friendships, and ability to 'fit in' to new groups and to manage relationships with new peers and new teachers. This will be in addition to understanding the different expectations made upon them by others and knowing how to present themselves to others whom they have not met before. A most useful framework for trainee teachers to understand how transitions impact on children was offered some years ago by Jadue-Roa and Whitebread (2012), who identified the following three approaches to understanding transitions:

> *The first relies on the belief that a transition is a critical process that puts the person in risk of harm, because there is a lack of continuity that threatens the emotional and psychological well-being of the child ... the second is concerned with readiness for school and future success in academic activities ... The third approach acknowledges transition as part of the school life of a child. Young children's perspectives, voices and agency are sought, so that by empowering them in their own life experience processes, there is less risk of emotional distress and later negative impact on school success.*

> (pp32–3)

It must be remembered that as children leave early years settings, they may also leave behind established friendship groups, this as well as established relationships with significant adults who have laid down the foundations for much of their future learning and social and emotional development.

LEAVING PRIMARY SCHOOL

Later transitions, when children are leaving primary school for post-primary education, are typically characterised by feelings of excitement together with some apprehension, but for some children this can be a very challenging period in their lives (Chedzoy and Burden, 2005). Indeed, Lyons and Woods (2012) have suggested that as many as 25 percent of children making the transition from primary to secondary school can find the process to be problematic as, for example, when the 'lack of a strongly supportive peer group leaves children vulnerable during transition' (p9). In developmental terms, friendships at this stage have become extremely important as they provide important emotional and social support and help children to safely internalise constructs of the educational world they will be entering, and in which they will move through adolescence and on to adulthood.

— **KEY THEORY** ———————————————————————————————

Reflections on the first year in secondary school: some findings from a research study

Tobell (2003), cited in Choi (2012), undertook a study on 30 girls who were interviewed during their first year in secondary school. The girls tended towards viewing transitions less positively, pointing to difficulties with having fewer personal relationships and expectations upon them to demonstrate 'a sudden increase in responsibility as a young adult' (p27).

DOES PRESCHOOL SUPPORT SOCIAL DEVELOPMENT?

Two decades ago, Buckingham (2000) highlighted the changing nature of children's experiences in their early years when he drew attention to how children were spending less time with their parents and more in institutionalised settings, a trend that has continued to grow in the past two decades (MacBlain et al., 2017):

> *Even for those who live in traditional nuclear families, children spend decreasing amounts of time with their parents, and more in institutionalized child-care of some form; and they are also less likely to have siblings available for companionship.*

(Buckingham, 2000, p65)

Debate continues to surround the benefits of very young children spending increased amounts of time in institutionalised settings as opposed to being at home. The essence of this debate was recently captured in Taggart et al. (2015), published for the Department for Education (DfE), where it was reported that children at 5 years of age who had attended preschool had, in general, benefited from the experience, compared with those who had not. Duration of attendance was revealed to be important, with 'an earlier start (under 3 years) being related to better development for language, pre-reading, early number concepts and nonverbal reasoning' (p8), while longer 'duration (in months) also improved independence, concentration and sociability' (p8). Attending preschool part-time (half a day) was reported 'to be just as good as having attended full time' (p8). Key findings in the research brief can be seen in Figure 4.1.

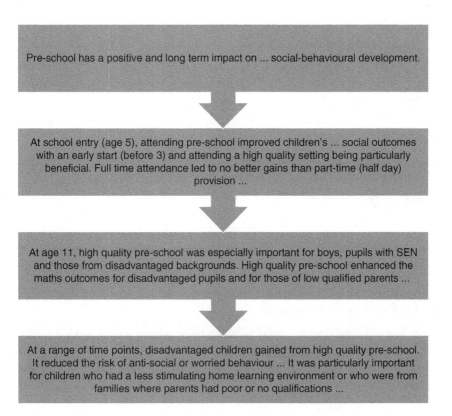

Figure 4.1   Key findings from Taggart et al. (2015)

Importantly, the research brief indicated that while preschool cannot eliminate the adverse effects of disadvantage, it can nevertheless ameliorate them. High-quality preschool was also seen as an important 'protective' factor for children from disadvantaged backgrounds. One very important finding was 'that having attended a high quality pre-school reduced the effects of multiple disadvantage on later attainment and progress in primary school' (p16).

ACTIVITY

View the following YouTube video: *Ages and Stages of Middle Childhood 6 to 12 Year Olds* (**www. youtube.com/watch?v=OtpiBtL_7zc**). How might Key Stage 1 and Key Stage 2 teachers implement strategies that support children in their social and emotional development?

CHAPTER SUMMARY

- Social development in every child is an individual and unique process that is shaped by internal as well as external factors.

- The nature of each child's moral development impacts on their social as well as academic progression.

- Trainee teachers need to appreciate and properly understand how environmental factors shape children's development and learning.

- Young children need to be supported by their teachers in developing strong self-efficacy, which will prepare them for later life.

- Social fears can be very real for some children and can have a significant impact on their development and learning.

- The role that teachers play in supporting children's social development is integral to meeting the standards required for Qualified Teaching Status (QTS) in the UK.

EXTENDED READING

Castrén, A. and Widmer, E. (2015) 'Insiders and outsiders in stepfamilies: adults' and children's views on family boundaries', *Current Sociology*, 63(1): 36–56. An interesting paper that offers insights into children's experiences of divorce and separation.

Cloughessy, K. and Waniganayake, M. (2014) 'Early childhood educators working with children who have lesbian, gay, bisexual and transgender parents: what does the literature tell us?', *Early Child Development and Care*, 184(8): 1267–80. This paper offers an analysis of some of the literature on working with LGBT parents in preschool settings.

Luke, I. and Gourd, J. (2018) *Thriving as a Professional Teacher*. London: Routledge. An excellent account of the professional challenges facing teachers entering the profession.

5
CHILDREN'S EMOTIONAL DEVELOPMENT

WHY YOU SHOULD READ THIS CHAPTER

It is only in recent decades that we have begun to properly recognise how emotional development and well-being affects children's learning. Teachers in training need to understand the complex nature of emotions in children, how emotions impact on children's learning, barriers that prevent well-being in children, and how schools can act as agents of change in supporting their pupils' emotional development.

By the end of this chapter, you should know:

- what characterises emotional development and well-being in children;

- how barriers distort children's emotional development and well-being;

- why good emotional intelligence is important for children's development and learning;

- why it is important for teachers to view children as holistic learners;

- how mental health impacts on children's learning and the need for strong resilience; and

- how to relate emotional development and well-being to the QTS standards.

INTRODUCTION

Teachers, when meeting a class for the first time, will be confronted with a set of unique individuals whose personalities have been, to a greater extent, already shaped by a complex dynamic involving genetics, physiological and environmental factors, and wider historical, cultural, economic and political influences. The judgements they make about each child's personality and their levels of emotional development and well-being will have enormous implications for how they then teach that child. Not only are teachers responsible for each child's academic progress, but they are also expected to play a fundamental role in supporting each child's emotional development and well-being; it is now expected of teachers that they give appropriate support to this aspect of children's development and the way in which it affects their learning. Whitebread (2012) has explained this as follows:

> *Within schools and other educational contexts, emotions are sometimes seen as a distraction, as an aspect of human behaviour which has to be coped with, but which is essentially irrelevant to the business of learning. In fact, everything we now know ... suggests that this is a misguided and potentially highly damaging view.*

(p15)

The important role that teachers play in supporting children's emotional development and well-being is well recognised and is clearly embedded in the standards set out for Qualified Teaching Status (QTS) in the UK, as indicated in the following standards, where QTS requires that teachers should:

— LINKS TO TEACHER STANDARDS ————————————————

- have a secure understanding of how a range of factors can inhibit pupils' ability to learn, and how best to overcome these (A5);

- know how to adapt teaching to support pupils' education at different stages of development (A5); and

- have a clear understanding of the needs of all pupils ... and be able to use and evaluate distinctive teaching approaches to engage and support them (A5).

(DfE, 2012)

WHAT EMOTIONAL DEVELOPMENT AND WELL-BEING LOOKS LIKE

From birth, children develop at an astonishing rate, not only physically, but also emotionally; as they do so, they must learn how to adapt to events in their lives and to the changing nature of the environments around them. Subsequent transitions from home to early years settings and then primary school will present a significant challenge for many children, though for others these will be approached with great enthusiasm and much excitement. Some children can feel very vulnerable during periods of transition as they see elements of their environments that have defined their security changing, and in ways that are beyond their control (see earlier discussion in Chapter 4). As children make these transitions and grow and mature, they will need stability and consistency in their lives, and importantly emotional nurturing from primary caregivers, as was so well articulated some years ago by Curran (2012):

> If a child is in an environment where they are understood as an individual human being then ... Their self-esteem will be improved, and ... If their self-esteem is good they will gain self-confidence ... If they are in an environment where their self-esteem is good and they have self-confidence, they will feel engaged with that environment. And what does all that add up to? Well, love as it happens.

(p5)

— CRITICAL QUESTION ————————————————————

What steps can primary schools take to support children transitioning from early years settings who are anxious and even fearful about their transition? Is it enough for teachers in primary schools to simply distract these children from their anxieties and tell them not to be anxious, or should they be doing more and, for example, spending some discrete time with their parents to learn more about why they might be anxious and fearful?

How children express their emotions when they first begin primary school will reflect their immaturity, and this will, of course, vary from one child to another; what might upset one child could, for example, be a huge source of fun and great excitement for another. At this age, children will also experience some difficulties with understanding and expressing their own feelings; for some, this can present as a significant problem. Drawing upon the work of Sigmund Freud (referred to later), Mercer (2018) has indicated how children, during the primary school years, or the *latency period*, as Freud called it, may have intense emotional lives but may be 'less expressive' of their feelings and emotions. Teachers need to be mindful, for example, that a child who continuously presents as being extremely quiet and biddable might actually be suppressing difficult emotions and feelings that they have learned to disguise but that define many aspects of their thinking and how they relate to others around them. Mercer (2018) has illustrated this point clearly, as follows:

> *Anger, fear, and pleasure are all related to a child's thinking and beliefs about the world, especially the social world ... a child's theory of mind helps to determine whether he or she will respond with emotion to the actions of another person that may or may not be intentional.*

(p149)

Importantly, Mercer (2018) goes further in emphasising how the changing emotional reactions of children during this period are 'also connected with success in developmental tasks such as school work, sports, peer relationships, and family relationships' (p150). The following 'descriptions' now offer approximations of typical characteristics of emotional development in children during their primary years at school. Clearly, these are not exact descriptors of children's development at the ages given, and it should be understood that children will present differently and with different abilities at different ages. Teachers therefore need to reflect carefully on the judgements they make about children's abilities and potential, and not rush into making decisions and sharing these with colleagues and parents about the individual learning abilities of their pupils.

THE PRIMARY YEARS: KEY STAGE 1

Referring to the transition from early years to primary school at age 5 years, Cowie (2012) has emphasised how children mostly learn to regulate their emotions informally as a way of managing relationships with those around them and the 'ups and downs of everyday life' (p18). When children first enter primary school, they soon learn that the sort of behaviours accepted from toddlers may not be acceptable in school.

At 5 years of age, as they enter primary school, children typically respond very well to consistency and stability and feeling safe. This said, they may have some difficulty in viewing things from the point of view of others and in expressing their emotions and feelings in words. Repetition of activities offers security and is an important feature of their learning. They learn that they can predict outcomes, an example of which is when children ask to hear the same story over and over many times when they already know how the story ends. Having opportunities to explore, touch and handle objects is also very important at this age and provides opportunities for children to safely explore new environments, a feature of learning in young children that has been recognised for generations by such notable theorists, philosophers and practitioners as Froebel, Montessori and Steiner.

At around 6 years of age, when children move into Year 1 of their primary school, teachers will observe them to be more motivated in their learning and to enjoy engaging in activities for the sake of doing them. This sense of motivation is an important element in their learning and in their emotional development and will set the foundations for future learning. They will also be developing a better understanding of the past and events that might occur in the future and will be showing signs of increasing competitiveness. Teachers may, for example, observe their pupils at this stage striving to finish first with their work, wanting to be first in a race and wanting to be at the front of a queue; their pupils will also respond well to praise and encouragement from adults. Cowie (2012) has alerted us to how children at this age may understand that while another child appears happy, they may in fact not actually be happy; they may even have a sense that the other child does not want their peers to know how he or she is feeling (p18). Children at this age can also become very easily upset, and it will be important that their teacher understands what is causing them to be upset, what factors are triggering the upset and how the child is trying to cope with their upset. For some children, this will be extremely important, as they may have already learned to hide and disguise their feelings, even from adults.

At around 7 years of age, children will continue to enjoy repetition, though at times they will want to work alone, and especially on activities that interest them. This is an important feature of their development as it indicates that they are becoming more independent and are gaining in confidence and self-reliance. Being able to work independently will be important as teachers and the demands of the curriculum increasingly expect and demand individual application from pupils. Vocabulary will continue to develop at a rapid pace, and importantly this will provide children with the means of expressing their feelings, disappointments, anxieties, and so on in more accurate and meaningful ways. Children may, however, become anxious about getting things wrong and making errors in their work. It will be important for teachers then to work with children who are experiencing such anxieties to prevent feelings of low self-esteem and low self-confidence developing, so that children at this young age do not come to internalise feelings of self-doubt and images of themselves as being 'not very able'. If children are left to experience failure and not given adequate strategies to overcome challenges presented by their academic work (for discussion of strategies, see Chapter 6), then sadly they will come to believe that they are simply 'not very able'. One sees this so often in older children who, had they been given appropriate strategies in their learning when younger, would not have convinced themselves that they are 'no good at schoolwork' and 'not very bright'. Children at this age respond well to reassurance from their teachers and to having clear structures in their day and school week.

THE PRIMARY YEARS: KEY STAGE 2

At around 8 years of age, teachers may observe some children as they grow in their ability to work independently, rushing too quickly when starting tasks and activities; these children will need to be reminded to take their time and to think about what is being asked of them and what they need to do to achieve the desired outcome; to not do so may mean that they experience persistent failure and may even come to be demotivated and lose confidence in their abilities to achieve success. Children at this age will enjoy lots of physical activity, be more sociable with others and be able to manage feelings better. They will enjoy being given responsibilities, such as tidying their teacher's desk or a cupboard, and will generally have a larger number of friends. They will be more competitive.

At around 9 years of age, children may be observed to demonstrate greater competitiveness outside of the classroom when playing games and even to be critical of the actions of their peers. They will take greater pride in their accomplishments and finishing tasks well and will pay more attention to detail. Children at this age can generally manage conflict better than before, though this might not be the case for all children of this age. As they become more independent, they will seek relationships outside of their family but will also need the security of the family when feeling insecure. Though they are also still heavily influenced by their parents and primary caregivers, they may have a strong desire to belong to a particular group. While this may be a good thing, it can also present difficulties, depending, of course, on the nature of the group. When part of a group, they may be more vulnerable to pressure from others within the group and may, for example, become pressurised into doing things they know are wrong. They may appear moody at one moment and then quickly appear OK.

At around 10 years of age, children may be observed to become quickly upset with other children but will also be quick to forgive others. They will generally work well in group activities and situations, enjoy talking with their peers, and also want to talk a lot. They will concentrate for longer and seek to explore the nature of their friendships and their relationships with peers and will manage disappointment better. Children at this age have a clearer sense of themselves and who they are. As girls are developing faster than boys, they will be experiencing a whole range of emotions, many of which they will not properly understand and that are new to them; they may, for example, be easily embarrassed and feel anxious about events and aspects of relationships with their peers. At times, teachers may observe children at this age being quite volatile, though they typically can manage their emotions better.

At around 11 years of age, as the onset of puberty occurs, children may have mood swings and test adults to their limits. Parents may report to their teachers that their child can be cruel to younger brothers or sisters at home and is increasingly argumentative. Fears from earlier childhood may resurface and cause them some anxiety, and though they may want to appear grown-up, they will not want to be 'babied' and may resist being helped by parents when with their peers. At this age, they may have a strong tendency to question why they should be learning material that they feel is irrelevant to them and may prefer to engage in learning activities that they feel have a clear purpose. They will expect high standards of behaviour from others and have a strong sense of fairness and of right and wrong and have huge ambitions, such as wanting to fly helicopters or become an astronaut or a famous celebrity.

▬ KEY THEORY

Erik Erikson and psychosocial development

One theoretical approach that has offered much to our understanding of children's emotional development is that of the celebrated psychologist Erik Erikson (1980), who viewed the course of normal development as moving through eight stages. His *Theory of Psychosocial Development* proposed that individuals need to move successfully through each stage in order to develop healthy personalities. The first four stages are most relevant to teachers working with children in the primary years.

(Continued)

(Continued)

Stage 1: trust versus mistrust (birth to 18 months)

Children are developing trust in the world around them, and particularly their carers. Trust is largely dependent upon the nature of the consistency and reliability of the care received. Children who receive consistent and reliable care then carry this into their own future relationships and develop a strong sense of security. If their care lacks consistency and reliability, children learn to mistrust and will carry this into their future relationships, together with associated anxieties.

Stage 2: autonomy versus shame and doubt (18 months to 3 years)

Children are developing independence and autonomy and putting physical distance between themselves and caregivers. They learn that they have choices about what to eat and how to play. Parents play an important role in supporting growth towards independence and giving opportunities to achieve success and develop self-esteem, self-confidence and self-efficacy. Successful progression through this stage leads to confidence and security. Unsuccessful progression, where, for example, children are overly disciplined or 'put down' by adults, can lead to overdependence on others in later life and feelings of self-doubt and low self-esteem.

Stage 3: initiative versus guilt (3 to 5 years)

Children are beginning to develop a sense of purpose. Language is improving and children are developing their capacity to empathise with others. Over-control at this stage can result in feelings of guilt, which may present as a lack of initiative. Children ask lots of questions, and if their requests are unheeded then they will not have been given the appropriate status. Feelings of guilt, accompanied by embarrassment and even shame, may follow and may result in the child reducing the degree to which they seek to interact with others. Difficulties at this stage may become linked to a reduction in creativity.

Stage 4: initiative versus inferiority (5 to 12 years)

Children are now attending primary school and their learning has become more formal in nature. Their teacher and peer group have become important role models and will guide much of the child's own activities. Winning the approval of their peers is important, as, through this, children develop a sense of pride in who they are, as well as in what they can do. Successful progression leads to children developing feelings of confidence in their ability to succeed and to be industrious. Unsuccessful progression may result in feelings of inferiority and self-doubt. During this stage, children develop their sense of competence.

BARRIERS TO EMOTIONAL DEVELOPMENT AND WELL-BEING

Barriers to emotional development and well-being in children are many and can present in a variety of forms, which all too often go unrecognised and hidden throughout childhood and even adulthood; poverty, neglect and abuse, early experiences of loss/bereavement, and poor nutrition may all play a part.

While emotional development in the majority of children's lives is characterised by stability, love and affection, the reality is that for many, this simply is not the case (MacBlain et al., 2017; Ofsted, 2015; Senior, 2016). Teachers therefore may find themselves faced with having to manage the learning of pupils whose emotional development is at best immature and at worst delayed and even disordered, due to neglect in their early years, an absence of stability in their lives and poor role-modelling by primary caregivers. In extreme cases, emotional development may have been arrested by dreadful events that were witnessed and even experienced by the children themselves. Such developmental issues will almost certainly have a significant and detrimental impact on children's learning as they progress through school.

Less than a decade ago, Cowie (2012) drew attention to how children growing up today face levels of severe stress that would have been unknown even a generation ago, with thoughts of suicide being 'common among young people', and this in addition to 'feelings of hopelessness and futility' (p2). Cowie also alerted us to how each year in the UK, around 100,000 children run away from home or from care, with around a quarter of this number doing so before the age of 13 and one in ten running away before the age of 10. Cowie also reported how in 2012 alone, the National Society for the Prevention of Cruelty to Children (NSPCC) dealt with over 30,000 cases. A review by the NSPCC (Cuthbert et al., 2011) found that in 2010, some 20,000 infants in the UK below 1 year of age were living with a parent using Class A drugs and over 93,000 infants in the same age range were living with a parent who was a problem drinker. Again, Cowie (2012) alerted us to some extremely worrying statistics when she indicated how some '200 UK children die each year as a result of direct or indirect abuse by their parents', and that 'child abuse is the fourth commonest cause of death in pre-school children' (p2). Cowie (2012) goes on to indicate how those children who have experienced abuse and neglect during their preschool and primary years often continue to experience significant emotional and social problems:

> For those who survive, the outcomes include increased risk by the time of adolescence of depression, eating disorders, drug misuse and involvement in crime and violence. By adolescence, children who have been abused or neglected by their parents are more likely to … find the process of parenting a challenging experience.

(pp2–3)

CRITICAL QUESTION

To what extent do you think teachers need to understand all aspects of safeguarding for children?

Barriers that impact on children's development and well-being continue to present significant challenges not only for the children themselves, but also for their teachers, who may be tasked with providing environments in which children can feel safe and secure and which support their learning and academic progress. Recently, Hope (2018), for example, alerted us to how the emotional development and well-being of children continues to be a case for concern and a feature that must lie at the heart of how teachers in their professional practice effectively support their pupils, when she reported how 'the life satisfaction of children in England was rated the lowest of 14 countries excluding South

Korea' (p25), and cited Roffey (2016), who reminds us that 'for some children school may be the only place where people authentically care about them' (p39). Such an assertion has clear implications for how teachers support the emotional development of children, and importantly how school managers also support their teachers in doing so. Hope draws further on the work of Roffey (2016), stressing how 'one of the pivotal protective factors she [Roffey] identifies in helping children to develop the resilience they need to cope with difficult circumstances, is the role of a caring teacher' (Hope, 2018, p30). The phrase 'a caring teacher', however, requires further analysis, for although it is true to say that teachers are caring, not all teachers may be caring in the true sense of the word.

▬ KEY THEORY

Do all teachers really care?

The American philosopher Nel Noddings (Infed, 2018) sees the main aim of education as that of creating caring, confident, loving and lovable individuals. Noddings has drawn an interesting distinction between two types of caring. Most teachers, she suggests, care in the 'virtue' sense (i.e. they will be conscientious in what they do, following goals and objectives for their pupils and working hard to inspire them to reach goals and do well academically). However, she also proposes that some teachers 'may be unable to establish relations of care and trust' in what she terms a 'relational sense'. This is where they bring to their teaching high levels of empathy and where they view each child as a wholly unique individual. She suggests that some teachers may find difficulty in accepting this idea of relational caring because of a strong legacy in teaching where teachers feel they know best, which she challenges, emphasising that such a view is now unacceptable. Noddings has also emphasised the type of challenges facing teachers in classrooms today, pointing towards the complex nature of some children's conditions, external factors such as large class sizes, the nature of the curricula that teachers have to follow, and requirements placed on teachers to frequently test children and achieve targets.

Interestingly, Noddings draws attention to how external factors, such as the *requirements placed on teachers to test children and achieve targets*, can influence the practice of teachers. This is a point also taken up by Hope (2018), who has emphasised how teachers in the UK might struggle to maintain a balance between the demands of delivering a target-driven curriculum and having to meet the emotional and social needs of their pupils:

> The need to maximize every moment of potential learning time can lead to classrooms that minimize the human needs of teachers and learners and pressurize both leading to anxiety, stress and potential unhappiness.

(p25)

CHILDHOOD NEGLECT AND ITS IMPACT ON DEVELOPMENT AND LEARNING

Sadly, many children grow up in homes where their emotional development is affected by having to witness and even experience physical abuse. It has been estimated (Walker et al., 2009) that domestic violence accounts for some 14 per cent of all violent incidents in England and Wales. It has also been reported (Cawson, 2002) that some 6 per cent of children are maltreated by their parents or carers, with 7 per cent being subjected to serious physical abuse. Worryingly, an estimated 6 per cent of children have experienced serious absence of care during childhood, with a similar number experiencing frequent and severe emotional maltreatment (Colverd and Hodgkin, 2011).

Some children entering primary school, therefore, will have already internalised models of adult behaviour that may prevent them from placing trust in their teachers and other adults they meet in school. These children bring with them repressed memories that can suddenly surface during learning activities, distracting them from their learning and even influencing how they relate to their teacher and peers. Claxton (2005) has spoken of even very young children having an 'emotional apprenticeship' in which they observe how important adults manage their emotions. Here, Claxton draws an important connection between these observations:

> When uncertain how to respond emotionally to a new person or event, babies and toddlers take their cue from the facial expression and tone of voice of the people they trust ... Whether deliberately or inadvertently, family members act as powerful role models that steer the child's emotional development ... Being around an adult who continually 'loses it' is bad for a child's own emotional development.

(p20)

To understand how children at different stages of their development experience feelings, we now turn to a relatively recent contribution to our knowledge of children's emotional development, that of *emotional intelligence* or, as some refer to it, *emotional literacy*.

EMOTIONAL INTELLIGENCE AND LEARNING

It is now recognised that children's emotional intelligence impacts greatly on their learning (Goleman, 1996; Hope, 2018). Emotional development in children requires that, even from their first months, they are supported in learning how to recognise their own emotions and those of others, understanding how their emotions arise, and importantly learning how to manage their emotions. By doing so, children greatly enhance their opportunities to engage purposefully with others and with the demands of the learning situations their teachers present to them. This process has been described as emotional intelligence (Salovey and Mayer, 1990) and is sometimes referred to as emotional literacy (Goleman, 1996). Salovey and Mayer (1990) defined emotional intelligence as that 'subset of social intelligence that involves the ability to monitor one's own and others' feelings and emotions, to discriminate among them and to use this information to guide one's thinking and actions' (p189).

Salovey and Mayer (1990) suggested four factors that are central to the development of emotional intelligence: *perceiving*, *reasoning*, *understanding* and *managing* emotions. As young children develop, they observe and begin to comprehend, with increasing accuracy, the emotions of others. They do this by becoming more sensitive to how others around them behave and by making interpretations of the facial expressions of adults, in addition to interpreting their body language. In this way, children gain a deeper understanding of what certain patterns of behaviour might mean; importantly, they also become attuned to the power of their own spoken language as well as that of others.

As this process develops, children engage with their own emotions, and in doing so they extend their intellectual and cognitive abilities. Children increasingly attach meaning to emotions as they make interpretations of them, and in doing so they learn to manage their own emotions. Trainee teachers need to recognise that when this process works well, it can facilitate and progress new learning in children, but when it does not children may experience emotional uncertainty and even chaos, which can present significant challenges to their teachers, who are tasked with ensuring good standards of behaviour and effectively supporting their pupils' well-being, both of which are key to meeting the UK QTS standards.

▬ KEY THEORY

Understanding children's emotional responses: a useful framework

Drawing on the original work of Mayer (co-author with Salovey referred to earlier), Goleman (1996, p48) indicated how Mayer had suggested that individuals fall into distinctive styles when attending to and dealing with their emotions (Figure 5.1).

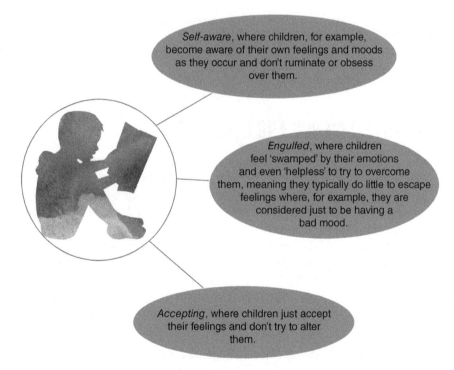

Self-aware, where children, for example, become aware of their own feelings and moods as they occur and don't ruminate or obsess over them.

Engulfed, where children feel 'swamped' by their emotions and even 'helpless' to try to overcome them, meaning they typically do little to escape feelings where, for example, they are considered just to be having a bad mood.

Accepting, where children just accept their feelings and don't try to alter them.

Figure 5.1   Distinctive styles when attending to and dealing with emotions

Such styles of responding to emotions clearly impact not only on the children themselves, but also on a teacher's ability to manage their behaviours and how these affect the dynamics of the whole class. Using the above descriptions offered by Goleman can provide teachers with a most useful means by which they can begin to understand their pupils' behavioural responses to events in their lives. Importantly, these descriptions provide teachers with a currency by which they can explain their pupils' behaviours to other teachers and external professionals. The descriptors therefore provide a means by which teachers can identify specific areas of a child's emotional functioning that they wish to target in order to support the child with developing their emotional intelligence.

VIEWING CHILDREN AS HOLISTIC LEARNERS

Central to trainee teachers having a clear understanding of the individual learning needs of each child is the necessity for teachers to also view children's development holistically. Though the importance of holistic learning in children has been recognised for generations and can be located in the ideas of such notable figures as Maria Montessori, Rudolf Steiner, John Dewey, Jerome Bruner, Urie Bronfenbrenner and many others, it has not always received the level of attention it deserves (MacBlain et al., 2015).

LEARNING IS A MULTILAYERED PROCESS

Importantly, holistic learning values the importance of purposeful and meaningful learning outside as well as inside of the classroom; it is child-centred and emphasises the importance of children becoming creative, critical and independent learners who place high value on themselves as individuals and others. Rose and Wood (2016) have acknowledged the complex nature of children's learning, explaining it as 'a holistic and multi-layered process affected by shifting and interacting multiple layers of influence' (p86). More recently, Hope (2018) encapsulated the importance of teachers adapting their teaching to meet the holistic needs of their pupils when she proposed that:

Ultimately, a teacher's responsibility is to nurture her students, by recognizing their potentiality and by not conflating a child's potentiality with ability groups or over-identifying a child with limited labels.

(p36)

DEVELOPMENTAL MATURITY AND HOLISTIC LEARNING

Holistic learning should be viewed as a nurturing process through which children not only develop their academic knowledge and skills, but also their social and emotional selves. The skills acquired by children as they develop alter with their levels of maturity and reflect the wider life experiences they have in their families and communities; these skills will, of course, contribute to how they later serve their own families and communities and become active and purposeful members of society. It is important, therefore, that during their formative years, children are actively supported by teachers in properly understanding their potential. Learning, after all, should be understood as a lifelong progression with transitions at different stages of children's lives.

LEARNING THROUGH THE DEVELOPMENT OF RELATIONSHIPS

A fundamental part of this progression is how children learn through the many relationships they experience over the course of their lives; it is through relationships that children develop their competencies and skills and better understand their own abilities and potential and feel confident in all they do. It is important, therefore, that teachers in the primary years develop professional relationships with their pupils that support them with their emotional development. By doing so, they will come to know their pupils better, be clearer about what motivates them in their learning, and what anxieties, if any, they have about approaching new learning activities and tasks.

▬ CASE STUDY 5.1

Factors that inhibit learning – adapting one's teaching

Gemma is on her final placement as a trainee teacher and has begun working in a Key Stage 1 class. When reading the class teacher's file notes, she learns that three pupils in her class have experienced significant emotional difficulties in the past. A key feature of her training at university so far has been the importance of gaining a clear understanding of the needs of all pupils, having a secure understanding of the factors that inhibit their learning, and knowing how to evaluate and adapt her teaching approaches to support pupils at different stages of their development, which are all part of the QTS standards she is working towards meeting. Gemma has also been studying the work of the theorist Nel Noddings, who has made her aware of two factors that she feels she needs to apply to her teaching while on placement in order to support these children.

First, she is aware that she needs to actively listen to them, and not simply just hear them, when they talk about themselves. In this way, she feels she might gain their trust, which will form the basis of the relationship she will have with them over her coming placement. Second, she will aim to be cooperative with these pupils when engaged in learning tasks and refrain from interfering when they appear absorbed in an activity or when actively collaborating with their peers.

As her placement begins, Gemma starts to engage with her pupils in dialogue as a means of learning more about their individual needs, in particular their strengths as opposed only to their weaknesses. In this way, she feels she is developing her teaching in a way that will help these children see the actual value of what she is hoping to achieve with them.

▬ CRITICAL QUESTION

What evidence might Gemma collect to demonstrate to her class teacher and her tutors that she is working towards meeting the QTS standards?

▬ ACTIVITY

View the following YouTube video: *Nel Noddings Theorist Film* (**www.youtube.com/watch?v= RrBpZFdeoVE**). Then list those factors you consider that contribute to good levels of 'care' in young children, giving priority to those you feel to be most important.

MENTAL HEALTH: ITS IMPACT ON DEVELOPMENT AND LEARNING

Though we know that children's development and learning is affected by their mental health, this is an area that has only, until recently, received little attention. The importance of mental health in children's development and learning was highlighted some years ago in a UK report produced jointly by Ofsted and the Care Quality Commission (CQC), *What About the Children?* (Ofsted, 2013b), which indicated how one in six of the adult population, around 9 million individuals, experienced problems with their mental health, with an estimated 30 per cent having dependent children between 0 and 18 years of age. The report went further in drawing evidence from a number of studies of individuals with health problems to indicate how at least 25 per cent of adults, and particularly young women, in acute psychiatric hospital settings could be parents. The report referred to previous findings from the NSPCC (Cuthbert et al., 2011), which estimated that 144,000 children below 1 year of age lived with a parent with a 'common mental health problem'. The report also drew findings from the National Treatment Agency for Substance Abuse (2011), which had collected information on the number of individuals using drug and alcohol services, which had estimated that some 200,000 adults were being treated for problems with substance misuse, with a particular concern being that nearly a third of these individuals were parents of children who lived with them. The review undertaken by the NSPCC (2011) also estimated that in 2010, nearly 20,000 children below the age of 1 year were living in a home where their parent was a user of Class A drugs and over 93,000 children in the same age range were living in a home with a parent who was recognised as a problem drinker.

CRITICAL QUESTION

What steps might a Key Stage 1 teacher take when a pupil discloses that he or she has watched their mother regularly taking Class A drugs?

A report by Childline (NSPCC, 2014) indicated how in 2012/13, they had received 2.4 million approaches, and that in 2013 they had offered counselling to 278,886 children and young people, with 10,961 children expressing to them concerns about another child. Regarding children below the age of 11 years, Childline reported the following very worrying facts:

- There were 22,733 counselling sessions with this age group.

- Some 86 per cent of young people within this age group were aged between 9 and 11.

- The youngest recorded age was 5, for which there were 319 counselling sessions.

- Nearly one in four (24 per cent) children aged 11 and under who contacted Childline during 2012/13 were concerned about bullying.

- Counselling about physical abuse was proportionately higher (9 per cent) for this age group, compared with 12–15-year-olds (6 per cent) and 16–18-year-olds (3 per cent).

- There was also a 19 per cent growth in counselling about school and education problems among this age group.

- A third (33 per cent) of neglect counselling was with children aged 11 and under.

- When a child describes their life to Childline, they rarely recognise that what they are experiencing is neglect.

Many children who have been struggling with depression and unhappiness have approached Childline, who, in 2012, established this as a new 'concern category', which included those children who were feeling sadness and loneliness, low self-esteem and low confidence, and concerns about their body image. More recently, the Mental Health Foundation (2018) reported that '70% of children and young people who experience a mental health problem have not had appropriate interventions at a sufficiently early age'. Action for Children (2018) also reported that 850,000 children in the UK have mental health problems.

RESILIENCE AND WELL-BEING

Bending (2018) has explained resilience as 'a dynamic process, in which an individual positively adapts and responds to risk, adversity and challenge' (p119). She goes on to empathise how some children overcome some hazards they encounter but others will 'falter'. Drawing upon the work of Rutter (2006), Bending (2018) goes on to suggest that resilience is 'a positive function that enables individuals to utilize coping strategies' (p119), and stresses that resilience is an acquired trait that children learn through their interactions with those social environments in which they live and grow up. Bending (2018) recognises, however, that there can be wide variations between how different children react to the same stressor, and notes that resilience depends on protective factors, which she describes as elements in children's social environments that 'support the use of coping skills, encourage autonomy, offer choice and control and provide the individual with a sense of community or connectedness to others' (p119). In terms of well-being, Bending (2018) has explained this as 'a multifaceted construct which indicates an individual's sense of happiness, satisfaction and meaning in life', and emphasises how chronic and long-lasting stressors are more likely to damage children than 'sudden extreme events' (p115). She includes among chronic stressors for children poverty and low economic status, both of which can reduce opportunities for children to socially integrate with their peers, violence in the home, neglect, and emotional and sexual abuse, which often lead to children withdrawing and becoming isolated. Bending (2018) goes on to emphasise how children spend 25 per cent of their day in school, and therefore the role that school plays in the management of children's emotional development is highly significant; she offers the following example:

> A child in school with little autonomy and control over their choice of peers or friendships is likely to have a lower sense of wellbeing than a child who feels connected to their school, part of a community that has strong boundaries, clear expectations and the opportunity to influence the environment. Further to this, a child who is happy and has a positive sense of wellbeing is more likely to work towards reaching their academic goals ... and achieve academically.

(p116)

BEREAVEMENT IN CHILDHOOD

Just how bereavement in childhood impacts on children's development and learning is not well understood and has only recently begun to be properly examined (MacBlain and MacBlain, 2004; MacBlain et al., 2017); the result of this has meant that longer-term issues impacting on the learning and development of children who have lived through bereavement of a close family member have largely gone unrecognised. In 2016, the National Children's Bureau (NCB, 2016) drew on findings from the Childhood Bereavement Network (CBN), which had reported how in 2014, some 40,000 children and young people in the UK had experienced the death of a parent. Some years earlier, in 2012, the Children and Young People's Mental Health Coalition (CYPMHC, 2012) had drawn attention to how in an average classroom, ten children would have lived through the separation of parents, with one child experiencing the death of a parent (p4). The extent to which loss in the early years can affect children throughout later development and impact on some more than others was indicated by Goleman (1996) when he cited the work of the neuroscientist Joseph Le Doux, who had proposed how early 'emotional memories' can remain with children as they grow, and result in feelings of confusion and anger (p22). Such feelings, Le Doux proposed, could even have an adverse impact on how children form and manage relationships with others, and importantly with their learning:

> Le Doux turns to the role of the amygdala [the main area in the brain where signals triggered by epinephrine and norepinephrine arrive] in childhood to support what has long been a basic tenet of psychoanalytic thought: that the interactions of life's earliest years lay down a set of emotional lessons based on the attunement and upsets in the contacts between infant and caretakers. These emotional lessons are so potent and yet so difficult to understand from the vantage point of adult life because, believes Le Doux, they are stored in the amygdala as rough, wordless blueprints for emotional life. Since these earliest emotional memories are established at a time before infants have words for their experience, when these emotional memories are triggered in later life there is no matching set of articulate thoughts about the response that takes us over.

> (Goleman, 1996, p22)

On occasions, teachers may be taken aback by the emotional outburst of a child and may then search for direct or immediate causes as to why the outburst has just taken place, when in fact the level of the emotional outburst may have its origins in events that took place in the child's early life, such as when the child experienced a significant loss, which has not been appropriately dealt with.

CRITICAL QUESTION

While on placement in a school, a child in your class makes a sudden emotional outburst for no apparent reason. What might be the first question you ask yourself about their behaviour, and what questions might you later ask of the class teacher?

Young children may also lack the vocabulary or the intellectual maturity to understand their feelings and fail to comprehend how these may have arisen because of earlier memories. Over the years, their feelings may have been repressed, with the result that they experience a sense of emotional chaos in their thinking that can result in patterns of poor behaviour that their teachers may misinterpret, erroneously attributing the causes to other reasons, such as lack of concentration, laziness, naughtiness, an exaggerated need for attention and even having a 'bad attitude'. What is of interest, however, is why some children seem to cope quite well with very difficult emotional memories, such as loss of a parent in early childhood, and demonstrate much higher resilience, while others do not.

▬ KEY THEORY

Factors affecting resilience in children's development

The level of resilience in children varies considerably, and teachers will ask themselves why some children cope well with difficult challenges while others do not. Garmezy (1985) and Grotberg (1995) have identified what they consider to be 'protective elements' that are important factors in helping us understand resilience. Elements identified by Garmezy were *self-esteem*, *family cohesion* and *absence of discord*, in addition to *availability of external support*. Grotberg considered other elements, *personality factors*, *family and external support structures*, and the *child's own social and interpersonal skills*, along with the three important illustrations shown in Figure 5.2 (see Barnard et al., 1999, p57).

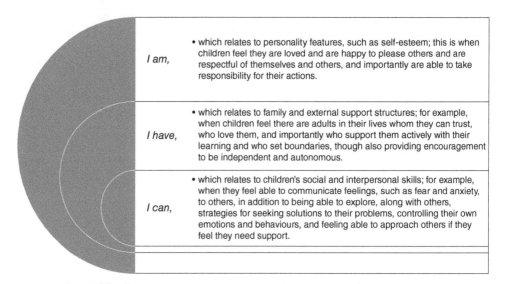

I am,	• which relates to personality features, such as self-esteem; this is when children feel they are loved and are happy to please others and are respectful of themselves and others, and importantly are able to take responsibility for their actions.
I have,	• which relates to family and external support structures; for example, when children feel there are adults in their lives whom they can trust, who love them, and importantly who support them actively with their learning and who set boundaries, though also providing encouragement to be independent and autonomous.
I can,	• which relates to children's social and interpersonal skills; for example, when they feel able to communicate feelings, such as fear and anxiety, to others, in addition to being able to explore, along with others, strategies for seeking solutions to their problems, controlling their own emotions and behaviours, and feeling able to approach others if they feel they need support.

Figure 5.2   Grotberg's protective elements

Importantly, Grotberg argued that it is possible to strengthen the first of these but not create them. With the second, she argued that it was possible to provide and strengthen these, though with the 'I can' factors she felt these have to be learned and cannot be taught. Grotberg also argued that when none of these protective elements are present in children's lives, then issues relating to poor mental health can ensue. It is important for teachers taking a class for the first time to acquaint themselves with any early losses experienced by their pupils and to understand that some pupils may have unresolved grief that presents as anger, difficulties sustaining relationships with others, and a lowering of self-confidence, but that may be misconstrued as 'bad' behaviour, poor concentration, and unwillingness to engage in activities and to collaborate with others. These unresolved feelings may also manifest themselves as low levels of self-efficacy where the children have come to see themselves as being of lower ability than their peers, and in more extreme cases as being 'not that able'. Teachers should endeavour to establish good positive working relationships with the parents of those pupils they might have concerns about and seek to meet with the parents on a regular basis to discuss any problems they think might be occurring; the earlier this is done, the better. Actively endeavour to develop skills in listening to children. Teachers should be open to empathising with pupils in a way that promotes trust so that they can talk about difficult emotional issues. Teachers should set aside time when they are free from distractions to listen to concerns being expressed by their pupils.

ACTIVITY

View the following YouTube video: *Ages and Stages of Middle Childhood 6 to 12 Year Olds* (**www.youtube.com/watch?v=OtpiBtL_7zc**). Then list those factors that influence development in the primary years. Should trainee teachers on placement support children with their social and emotional development?

CHAPTER SUMMARY

- Children are unique individuals whose emotional needs are created out of a complex interplay of hereditary factors that in turn are influenced by the environments in which they grow and develop.

- Teachers need to recognise how their practice impacts significantly on every child's emotional development, and how they learn.

- Teachers need to recognise how emotional development in children changes over time and how poor mental health and traumatic events can impact on children's well-being and learning.

- Schools should strive to ensure a healthy balance between delivering target-driven curricula and allowing teachers time to support emotional development in their pupils.

- The important role that teachers play in supporting emotional growth and well-being in children is now properly recognised and underpins the standards required for Qualified Teaching Status (QTS).

EXTENDED READING

Bending, H. (2018) 'Resilience in childhood', in I. Luke and J. Gourd (eds), *Thriving as a Professional Teacher*. London: Routledge. A very readable and informative chapter that draws upon psychological theory to explain resilience in children.

6

HOW BEHAVIOUR SHAPES DEVELOPMENT

WHY YOU SHOULD READ THIS CHAPTER

All behaviour is learned. It is essential that trainee teachers grasp this *concept* and understand that patterns of behaviour learned in early childhood shape many aspects of children's development and underpin much of their future learning. Likewise, trainee teachers also need to understand that their own behaviours will influence and even shape aspects of their pupils' development and how they engage subsequently in learning activities.

By the end of this chapter, you should know:

- that behaviour is highly complex and inseparable from children's development, their academic achievement and most aspects of their learning;

- that the term 'behaviour' should be used in critically informed ways that demonstrate deeper and accurate understanding of the whole child;

- that teachers, through their own actions, shape pupils' development and learning; and

- how to relate children's behaviours and their own actions to the QTS standards.

INTRODUCTION

> *Behaviour in school is inseparable from academic achievement, safety, welfare and wellbeing, and all other aspects of learning. It is the key to all other aims, and therefore crucial ... and should be viewed as an issue of the highest strategic importance. Behaviour does not manage itself, except haphazardly.*

> (Bennett, 2017, p12)

Unlike in previous generations, we now understand the importance of teachers understanding how behaviours learned in early childhood can impact on future development. Importantly, we also understand why teachers need to play an active role in teaching young children how to manage their behaviours, which is fundamentally different to exercising control in a classroom and disciplining children when they step out of line. Just over two decades ago, Fontana (1995) drew attention to how a lack of appropriate training had led to many teachers having a limited understanding of the complex nature of behaviour and the part they might play in supporting children with understanding and managing their own behaviours:

Teachers receive little training in social behaviour, and beyond the routine enforcement of the rules of politeness they often have limited expertise in this behaviour to pass on to children.

(p285)

Since Fontana's comments, there have been major strides in teacher training that now address the need for better understanding of the complexities of children's behaviour, as well as focusing on the management of behaviour. Whole rafts of research have now demonstrated how patterns of behaviour learned during the preschool and primary years impact on social and emotional development and are important determinants of future academic progress.

Schools in the UK must now have in place formal and transparent behaviour policies. When I (the author) worked as an educational psychologist in the 1990s in England, few schools had any such policies, and some had no policies other than vague agreements among staff about what to do when a child misbehaved. Policies today, however, need to be accessible to parents and pupils and should be made available to trainee teachers when on placement. A key function of these policies is to promote and ensure consistency of approach. The importance of having a consistent approach to behaviour management in children's first years of education and schooling is crucial, as it is through consistency that children develop their understanding of the expectations necessary for effective and purposeful learning in later and more formal settings, such as post-primary education. Indeed, Buckler and Castle (2014) recently emphasised this point by stressing how a key element of teaching in primary schools should be the need to ensure that:

the approach is consistent so that learners are aware of what is required and what is not deemed acceptable. This consistent approach needs to be developed as a whole school to avoid conflicting messages for learners. Furthermore, there also needs to be consistency in the way teachers make use of the approach.

(p292)

The importance of teachers supporting children in developing good patterns of behaviour is clearly embedded in the UK QTS standards, as indicated below, where teachers should:

LINKS TO TEACHER STANDARDS

- *have clear rules and routines for behaviour in classrooms, and take responsibility for promoting good and courteous behaviour both in classrooms and around the school, in accordance with the school's behaviour policy (A7);*

- *have high expectations of behaviour, and establish a framework for discipline with a range of strategies, using praise, sanctions and rewards consistently and fairly (A7);*

- *manage classes effectively, using approaches which are appropriate to pupils' needs in order to involve and motivate them (A7); and*

- *maintain good relationships with pupils, exercise appropriate authority, and act decisively when necessary (A7).*

(DfE, 2012)

UNDERSTANDING BEHAVIOUR IN THE CONTEXT OF DEVELOPMENT

While the term 'behaviour' is used almost daily by teachers to account for children's actions at different stages of their development and to report these in verbal or written forms, it is a term that is poorly understood (MacBlain, 2014). In a recent report that reviewed behaviour in schools in England, Bennett (2017) emphasised the importance of teachers fully understanding that when they use the term 'behaviour', they need to acknowledge the complexity of the term and understand it within a much wider context; Bennett explained the term 'behaviour', as used in schools, as:

> *any actions performed by any members of the student and staff communities. It includes conduct in classrooms and all public areas: how members work, communicate, relax and interact; how they study; how they greet staff; how they arrive at school, transition from one activity to another; how they use social media, and many other areas of their conduct. It does not merely refer to how students do or do not act antisocially.*

> (p12)

Schools, however, are characterised by their own unique cultures with mutually agreed ways of behaving that have evolved over years and that have become accepted and generally agreed by the adults who work there. Bennett's definition is therefore very helpful, as it emphasises how behaviour in schools should not just be seen as an issue for the pupils, but should instead be contextualised within the nature of the relationships and wider actions that take place every day between children, but should also include the actions of adults working in the school. Relationships are a key element in children's development, and it needs to be recognised that they are multifaceted and intricate, and at times difficult for some children to manage, especially those children whose emotional development is still at an immature level. It is important, therefore, that trainee teachers understand how from their first days in school, children have to learn to negotiate the complex and dynamic nature of relationships with a wide variety of adults, peers and older children. For those children who have benefited from guidance and appropriate experiences from parents and wider family members, this will be generally straightforward, but for some this may be extremely difficult.

EXPLANATIONS OF BEHAVIOUR: WHY ARE THEY DIFFERENT?

The term 'behaviour', as we have seen, is complex and demands great care when used in a professional context; it is helpful, therefore, to look at how theorists have sought to explain this aspect of children's development and how behaviour at different stages of development affects learning. When we look to theory for explanations, however, we find that they can differ significantly; this should not be seen as problematic, as no one theory can ever fully explain such a complex phenomenon. Rather, it should be understood that different theories can help us develop our understanding, and importantly inform our practice. A helpful starting point is to look at the theoretical ideas of the *behaviourists* that have contributed much to our knowledge of development in childhood, and how we might go about explaining children's behaviours and understanding their learning.

BEHAVIOURISM

This theoretical approach is founded on the view that associations develop between stimuli and responses and that these account for learning. *Behaviourists* argued that learning could be observed and explained in a systematic and objective manner through observation and experiment. Daniels and Shumow (2002) have explained the *behaviourist* view of children's development as follows:

> *a behaviourist view assumes that children do not develop on their own; rather development consists of learning sets of relatively passive responses to environmental stimuli, such as the teacher ... Beliefs associated with the behaviourist view include the ideas that children are not intrinsically motivated to learn what adults deem important.*

> (p505)

It should be recognised that *behaviourism* dominated much of the thinking and practice in schools in previous decades. In many respects, this was a reaction to earlier ideas about child development that had been promoted by *psychodynamic theorists*, whose ideas originated in the works of Sigmund Freud and focused largely on children's emotional development. Before looking more closely at the ideas of the *behaviourists*, it is important, therefore, to first understand the ideas of Freud and his followers (Susan Isaacs, Anna Freud and Eric Fromm, among others) against whom the *behaviourists* were reacting.

▬ KEY THEORY

Freud's legacy

Freud proposed that at the very core of individual development lie two determining elements, which are characterised by pleasure and by tensions. He further proposed that tensions in individuals arise from their sexual energy (the libido), with pleasure in individuals emanating from the release of this sexual energy; Freud used the term 'sexual' in a much broader manner to account for all those thoughts and actions that individuals find pleasurable (MacBlain, 2018). The work of Isaacs, however, focused predominantly on very young children who were at the 'nursery' stage of development and learning. Isaacs (1929, 1930, 1932) contributed a great deal to our understanding of early childhood, and not just through her attempts at applying psychoanalytic thinking, which had its origins in the ideas of Freud. Isaacs saw the role of adults working with young children in learning situations as central to their learning and saw adults as a very valuable resource. She believed that at the very heart of children's learning was the need to develop their emotions and feelings. This view of learning and development is very different to that of the *behaviourists*, as will be explained later. Isaacs also believed that children's learning environments should be viewed as an important resource where children were able to project their emotions. In this respect, her thinking was similar to that of Freud, who also emphasised the importance of environments that would allow individuals to project their inner emotions, and in some cases unresolved issues such as anger. Isaac believed in the importance of adult practitioners setting boundaries that were to be demonstrated as opposed to enforced, and with a clear emphasis on consistency; such an approach, she believed, was central to developing children's sense of security and safety. She also emphasised the importance of adults working with children having a comprehensive understanding of each child and argued that this could be achieved by adults engaging in careful and focused observation of children in different situations.

In stark contrast to the work of the psychodynamic theorists, the *behaviourists* placed far less importance on children's feelings and emotions, while emphasising the importance of observing and measuring children's actual behaviours and behaviour patterns. *Behaviourism* also contrasts with other theories that have sought to explain learning and child development as it focuses primarily on behaviours, with relatively little attention given to those complex 'inner processes' that take place within the brain and that we generally conceive of as 'thinking' and 'cognition'. Unlike the theoretical explanations proposed by Piaget and Freud, *behaviourism* did not view children as passing through stages of development. Papatheodorou and Potts (2016) have explained the *behaviourist* position succinctly, as follows:

> *In contrast to the Piagetian view, behaviourists saw learning as being the direct outcome of responses to environmental stimuli through a process of (positive and/or negative) reinforcement. According to this stimulus-response model, the child makes an association between a stimulus and the consequences that follow the triggered behaviour; a rewarding consequence is likely to increase the occurrence of the exhibited behaviour, while a punishing consequence would minimize it.*

> (p112)

Papatheodorou and Potts (2016) have also articulated the difference between *behaviourist* theory and sociocultural theories, such as those developed by Vygotsky, which challenged aspects of Piaget's theory as well as that of the *behaviourists*:

> *Vygotsky (2002) argued that development and learning take place within the social and cultural milieu: children are neither the lone scientists, isolated from their social environment (assumed in Piaget's theory), nor the product of direct stimuli of the environment and the process of positive or negative reinforcement (argued by behaviourists). Children are the product of their socio-cultural milieu, its beliefs and values, and its customs and practices.*

> (p114)

▬ ACTIVITY ▬

View the following YouTube video: *Teaching and Learning Approaches: Behaviorism, Cognitivism and Social Constructivism* (**www.youtube.com/watch?v=gkzLAz25KPI**), which explores differences between *behaviourism* and the ideas of other theorists, namely Piaget and Vygotsky.

The extent to which the *behaviourists* placed emphasis on the behaviours of children, and how these shaped development and future learning, can be seen in the original ideas of John Watson. In 1913, Watson (1928), who had established the school of *behaviourism*, which proposed that all behaviours are acquired through the process of conditioning, felt able to comment as follows:

> *Give me a dozen healthy infants, well-formed, and my own specified world to bring them up in and I'll guarantee to take any one at random and train him to become any type of specialist I might select – doctor, lawyer, artist, merchant-chief and, yes, even beggar-man and thief, regardless of his talents, penchants, tendencies, abilities, vocations and the race of his ancestors.*

> (p82)

Drawing upon the work of Watson, Burrhus Skinner (1951, 1953) emphasised how reinforcement can shape children's behaviours. Examples of positive reinforcement between a teacher and a child might be the teacher's smile or verbal praise when he or she is pleased with the child's actions. An often-seen practice in classrooms is the placing of stars on a chart when a pupil has successfully completed a task or demonstrated a desired behaviour. To gain a star, the pupil has to demonstrate a desired behaviour. In contrast, examples of negative reinforcement are where teachers use 'time out' when a child is being naughty. Teachers employ positive reinforcement to increase desired behaviours and negative reinforcement to 'extinguish' those behaviours that they do not want almost on a daily basis. In this way, teachers are active agents in shaping children's development, and therefore their learning.

REINFORCEMENT AND ITS IMPACT ON DEVELOPMENT

Skinner proposed that reinforcement that is positive strengthens the behaviours of individuals, and that the frequency with which reinforcement followed behavioural responses is an important factor in the increase of behaviours. Developing this idea further, he proposed a number of schedules of reinforcement that have informed the practice of teachers attempting to change the behaviours of pupils presenting with behavioural issues and conduct disorders. Skinner developed the notion of 'operant conditioning' based on his view that learning is not wholly a passive process, as was suggested by earlier *behaviourists*, but instead an active process. Operant conditioning holds that it is the learner that triggers changes in behaviour, and not the object, and that learning occurs when behaviours are rewarded or punished, in effect when associations are formed between behaviours and the consequences of those behaviours.

SHAPING DEVELOPMENT THROUGH CONSEQUENCES

Skinner argued that behaviours are shaped and sustained by their consequences – pleasant responses strengthen behaviours while unpleasant responses weaken behaviours, with the result that they diminish and are even extinguished. In simple terms, positive reinforcement strengthens learning while negative reinforcement diminishes it. Bigge and Shermis (2004) have suggested that while Skinner viewed the primary function of teachers as being that of transmitting culture, he also believed that 'the first task of teachers is to shape proper responses, to get children to pronounce and write responses properly', and the principal task of teachers 'as consisting of bringing proper behavior under many sorts of stimulus control' (p113). Bigge and Shermis (2004) have also cited the example of spelling, indicating that Skinner saw the teaching of spelling to be a 'process of shaping complex forms of behavior' (p113).

THE POTENTIAL OF COMPUTERS

Interestingly, Skinner viewed computers as a most effective and efficient resource for children's learning; children, he argued, could follow carefully designed programmes, which could then, at each new stage of learning, offer reinforcement through rewards. They could also break down learning into small steps, which would reduce the possibility of failure and increase the likelihood of success, thereby reinforcing the children's learning. In this respect, Skinner was very much ahead of his time. One only has to reflect on the impact that computers have made on children's learning, who are now able to get immediate answers to questions, store work assignments electronically, have the accuracy of their writing automatically checked, and access vast depositories of information; all of these have, of course, impacted on the social development of children and the way in which they think.

━ CASE STUDY 6.1 ━

Operant conditioning in action

Jenny has started her placement working with a new Key Stage 1 class. She has been told that a pupil named Dan is often the cause of disruption and that he tries to distract the other children and rarely attempts the activities set by the teacher. Jenny decides to try an intervention that she hopes will reduce Dan's undesirable behaviours. Jenny believes the main reason for Dan's undesirable behaviours is his need for attention. On her first day, Jenny sets the class a simple activity; she observes Dan becoming quickly absorbed in the activity and quite motivated. She goes straight to Dan while he is absorbed in the activity, and in a clear and soft voice she tells Dan that she is very pleased with his behaviour, which is 'working quietly' and 'doing what I asked you to do'. She smiles at Dan and then walks away. After a few minutes, she returns to Dan and again tells him that she is very pleased with him 'working quietly' and 'doing what I asked you to do'. After about ten minutes, she calls the class to attention, and in a clear and soft voice emphasises how pleased she is that they are all 'working quietly' and 'being attentive'. In this way, she is once again identifying those behaviours she is seeking to reinforce in Dan. Later on, in the morning session, she calls Dan over to her desk and again explains that she is very pleased with his behaviour, which is 'working quietly' and 'doing what I asked you to do'. Jenny continues to reinforce Dan's desired behaviours in this way by repeating this approach each day when asking the class to engage in different activities. By the end of her second week, she observes a significant change in Dan's behaviour. She recognises that rather than offering Dan attention when he is not on task, she will instead give him attention when he is actively engaged in an activity, and thereby reinforce his on-task behaviours by encouraging him when he is actively engaged through smiles and verbal praise.

━ CRITICAL QUESTION ━

View the behaviour policies of two primary schools you are familiar with and identify their key aims and what makes them different. Why are behaviour policies in some primary schools more effective than others? How might better training in the behaviour of children at different stages of development improve the practice of teachers entering the profession?

OBSERVING DEVELOPMENT THROUGH BEHAVIOURS

When on school placement, trainee teachers should take time to observe children's behaviours outside of the classroom as well as inside, and they should do so with purpose. It is important that they do so in ways that properly inform them; there is a fundamental difference between informed observations and simply watching what children are doing. Recently, Carter and Nutbrown (2014) encapsulated this important distinction when they emphasised how 'Watching young children can open our eyes to their astonishing capacity to learn, and make us marvel at their powers to think, to do, to communicate and to create' (p129). Trainee teachers should recognise, then, that when they qualify as teachers, they will have valuable opportunities each day to observe their pupils' behaviours, and in doing so learn a great deal about pupils' levels of development and how they best learn.

▬ CASE STUDY 6.2 ▬

An example of purposeful and meaningful observation

John is on his first school placement, and as part of his experience he has to observe a child who presents with behavioural problems. He stands in the playground at break time and focuses on the chosen child. He has made a checklist of behaviours to observe: how many times the child initiates contact with other individual children, how many times he initiates contact with groups of children, and how much time he actually spends by himself. He focuses solely on the task, trying to cut out any distractions, and is surprised to find that in a period of 20 minutes, the child does not initiate contact with any groups, but runs about pushing other children and then running off; his only verbal interactions are shouting. John subsequently finds that the child has been in care for most of his life and has moved from one foster parent to another. John then learns, through discussion with the class teacher, that this child has great difficulties in forming relationships with others, a factor that is due to early problems in bonding with parents and significant others when just an infant.

GIVING MEANING TO BEHAVIOURS

It is crucial for trainee teachers to understand that their interpretations of children's actions and the meanings they attribute to behaviours at different stages of development should be done with the upmost care and should be informed by careful observation and accurate assessment. To fail to do so may result in children being wrongly labelled, and in extreme cases stigmatised. An example of this is where a teacher might wrongly interpret a child's frequent off-task behaviours as being due to 'poor concentration', 'lack of motivation' or 'laziness', when in fact their cause may be located in undiagnosed conditions, such as attention deficit disorder or dyspraxia, which can cause problems with concentration and focusing attention. These children might then be described subsequently to future teachers as 'problem' children; this can also have a significant impact on how they develop socially, as they try to 'live up' to how they think their peers view them. Trainee teachers also need to appreciate how many of the behaviour patterns they observe in pupils will have been formed during their preschool years and mostly at home and may be continually reinforced by parents and significant others outside of school.

▬ CRITICAL QUESTION ▬

How might teachers find time to observe the behaviours of children inside their classrooms and how might they go about recording these?

CHILDREN'S DEVELOPMENT AND THE IMPORTANCE OF WORKING WITH PARENTS

While the vast majority of parents work in collaboration with their children's teachers, there are those who do not; this can cause major issues for those children who receive very conflicting messages about their behaviours from different key adults in their lives. It is most important, then, that trainee teachers fully understand the need to work in partnership with parents. By working collaboratively, it is more likely that teachers will be able to send strong messages to their pupils regarding expectations from others, boundaries and shared values. To fail to do so may mean that some children learn from an early age that their teachers' values and expectations conflict with those of their parents – this can be confusing and problematic for their emotional and social development. Take the following case, where an educational psychologist is meeting with the parents of John, who is aged 8 and who has been referred by his school to the psychologist because of his constant swearing in the classroom.

--- **CASE STUDY 6.3** --

Having shared understandings of children's behaviours

Psychologist: *Can you tell me about John's behaviour at home.*

Father: *What are you trying to say, that we don't look after him?*

Psychologist: *No, I only want to gain a picture of John's behaviours and when he is at school.*

Mother: *We run a restaurant, so we are very busy. I put him to bed after tea time and he then watches TV until he falls asleep. I make sure he is settled before I go down to work in the restaurant and I go up every so often to check he's fine.*

Psychologist: *A major concern at school is that he swears at his teacher when he gets angry. Does he ever swear at home?*

Father: *No, he doesn't swear at home.*

Mother: *Well, he did use to swear, but we quickly put a stop to that, and now, as his father says, he doesn't ever swear now.*

Psychologist: *What made him stop swearing at home?*

Mother: *Well, every time he swore, we smacked him really hard. He quickly learned that if he swore, that's what would happen. We don't need to do it anymore.*

The above example indicates how a school's way of managing behaviour is in direct contrast to that of the child's parents and home life. It is clear that John's parents have vastly different views as to how unacceptable behaviour should be managed; for them, 'punishment' should be extreme, and it is this type of thinking that can influence the social and emotional development of children. It is also clear that John's teacher will need to work more closely with his parents to establish agreed interventions for managing John's behaviours, and in doing so demonstrate clearly to John that his teacher and parents are working in close partnership with each other in consistently applying the same consequences to his behaviours. A major challenge for his teacher, however, will be the need to extinguish John's inappropriate behaviour of swearing and replace this with a different behaviour that is acceptable. It is likely that John will initially be resistant to this change, as he has learned this unacceptable response over time in his home and it will have been reinforced and strengthened by the responses he has had from his parents, which have clearly lacked sensitivity and understanding. John's teacher needs to insist with his parents that they stop this pattern of behaviour and replace the consequence of John's swearing with a more acceptable response, which they will then need to reinforce consistently.

INTERPRETING DEVELOPMENT: THE IMPORTANCE OF ACCURACY

Because children develop differently and at varying levels of quickness, it is essential that teachers training to enter the profession properly understand the importance of articulating and recording children's behaviours with accuracy and in ways that are precise, unambiguous and clear to intended recipients. This is especially important where perceptions of children's behaviours are written down and interpretations then made of these behaviours. Reports written on children in their primary years can remain with them for many years, and may influence how future teachers perceive their intellectual ability and potential, the drivers that have shaped their personalities and that cause them to behave in certain ways, and the academic groupings or 'sets' they will be placed in. The importance of teachers being precise when using the term 'behaviour' to describe children's actions and explain their thinking, therefore, is key to recording accurate statements about their pupils' learning.

Saying, for example, that a child's behaviour 'has greatly improved' might provide some general sense of change in the child, but it fails to provide any detail to an intended recipient. Such statements are vague and generally unhelpful and typically leave many questions unanswered, such as: What particular aspects of the child's behaviour have changed, and in what way? How has the child's thinking changed? Have new behaviours replaced undesired behaviours, and if so what are they? Equally, a teacher telling a young child that they 'need to improve their behaviour' may be relatively meaningless to the child as it offers little in the way of what the child must do, and yet we hear examples of such phrases being used daily by many teachers. Trainees entering the profession need to understand, therefore, that when they use the term 'behaviour', and perhaps more importantly when they use it in a written report to describe or explain children's actions, it should be used with specificity so that the intended reader knows precisely what is being said or inferred.

Some years ago, Fontana (1995) commented brilliantly on the subtlety of interactions in classrooms as follows:

> When the teacher talks to the child he or she receives a response which helps determine what is said next. The response may be verbal but may just as easily be non-verbal (e.g. facial expression, or shuffling feet). The thoughts and feelings it conveys may involve comprehension or incomprehension, interest, boredom, anxiety, hostility, amusement, or a host of other similar things, each of which influences the teacher's own thoughts and feelings in turn.

> (p288)

Importantly, Fontana (1995) goes on to suggest that while teachers will be aware they are having an interaction with a child, it is 'quite another [thing] to be able to analyse it in detail and decide where and how to change one's own behaviour in order to help change that of the child' (p288). Trainee teachers must guard against making interpretations about the interactions they observe in their classrooms, as these may disguise important and hidden aspects of children's development that are impacting on their learning and that present in other forms of behaviour that children use to mask difficult issues that they do not understand or know how to manage.

┌─── **ACTIVITY** ───

Take time to describe the behaviours you have observed in a child while on placement in a school with a fellow trainee, and then invite that trainee to relate back to you what they have learned about the child's behaviours from listening to you. Evaluate how specific your description was and how your use of language might have led the other trainee to have to ask for greater clarification.

└──

BEHAVIOUR: ISSUES AFFECTING DEVELOPMENT

Most teachers deal with low-level disruption, such as talking out of turn or distracting others, on a daily basis. While this is typically the case for many classroom interactions, there will be some children who present, even from their first years, with severe behavioural issues, which will impact negatively on their development and subsequent academic progress. Trainee teachers therefore need to understand that children who present with underlying disturbed behavioural patterns will require much greater support and understanding than the majority of their peers. Primary schools now have behavioural policies in place, and they have access to external agencies and other professionals, such as educational psychologists, behavioural support teams and school social workers, who can offer guidance and support as well as practical interventions. Supporting children and putting interventions in place as early as possible is crucial to their current and future development. Too many children enter secondary schools with complex social and behavioural difficulties that have failed to be recognised and properly addressed when they were younger, with the result that they may be excluded from school, become involved with crime, and fail to acquire the basics of literacy and numeracy that will enable them to realise their true potential as learners. The following section examines the nature of 'conduct disorders' in children, which can have an enormous impact on development and learning.

CONDUCT DISORDERS: THEIR IMPACT ON DEVELOPMENT

At times, teachers may have to deal with the behaviours of children with more complex behavioural conditions. One such condition is 'conduct disorder'. Less than a decade ago, a guide published by the Children and Young People's Mental Health Coalition (CYPMHC, 2012) aimed at supporting head teachers with preventing emotional and behavioural difficulties in children emphasised how pupils with conduct disorder and severe ADHD are more likely to experience marked difficulties with the acquisition of literacy and numeracy skills. The CYPMHC (2012) also drew an important distinction between conduct disorder, which they defined as 'a repetitive and persistent behaviour problem, where major-age-appropriate societal norms or the basic rights of others are violated', and emotional disorder, which, they suggested, refers to 'conditions such as depression and anxiety' (p4).

Teachers know that behavioural and emotional difficulties can impact negatively on the academic achievement of children, and this is particularly the case with persisting conduct or emotional disorders where pupils are also more likely to have special educational needs, and perhaps more worryingly face exclusion from their schools. Many of these pupils will leave school with few, if any, qualifications. It is also sadly the case that many children with conduct disorders later engage in substance abuse and go on to experience much higher levels of anxiety and depression than would be typical of their peers. It is now mostly accepted by professionals that interventions with children that involve their parents and immediate family members will be more likely to yield positive outcomes, especially if the interventions are put in place as early as possible in the lives of children. This has significant relevance for teachers of children in Key Stage 1 who are working with children in the early stages of their education and schooling, and perhaps are likely to work more closely with parents.

▬ KEY THEORY

Conduct disorders: how do they differ from poor behaviour?

Some years ago, Kring et al. (2013) made reference to the *Diagnostic and Statistical Manual of Mental Disorders* (DSM-5) when discussing conduct disorder, which they suggested focused on those sorts of actions that are illegal and that violate the rights of other individuals and break the consensus of agreed social norms. They also emphasised how, in meeting the criteria for being a conduct disorder, these actions have to be characterised by such factors as aggression and cruelty, lack of remorse and a degree of callousness, and high rates of frequency. They suggested that:

A related but less well understood externalizing disorder in the DSM-IV-TR is oppositional defiant disorder (ODD). There is some debate as to whether ODD is distinct from conduct disorder, a precursor to it, or an earlier and milder manifestation of it … Commonly comorbid with ODD are ADHD, learning disorders, communication disorders, but ODD is different from ADHD in that the defiant behavior is not thought to arise from attentional deficits or sheer impulsiveness.

(p407)

Kring et al. (2013) have also made reference to the work of Gerald Patterson and his colleagues, who developed and evaluated a behavioural programme, 'parent management training' (PMT), where parents of very young children were introduced to ways of modifying their responses to their children (p412). In particular, parents were encouraged to reward 'prosocial' as opposed to 'antisocial' behaviours in a consistent manner, or, as Kring et al. (2013) suggested, 'Parents are taught to use techniques such as positive reinforcement when the child exhibits positive behaviours and time-out and loss of privileges for aggressive or antisocial behaviours' (p412). Kring et al. (2013) went on to propose that though this type of programme had been modified over the years by others, it was in fact the 'most efficacious intervention' for children presenting with symptoms of conduct disorder and ODD (p412).

Addressing the need for schools to use consistent approaches to behaviour that are embedded in every aspect of the school, Bennett (2017) commented as follows:

The school must have well-established and universally known and understood systems of behaviour … Any area of general behaviour that can be sensibly translated into a routine should be done so explicitly. This removes uncertainty about school expectations from mundane areas of school life, which reduces anxiety, creates a framework of social norms, and reduces the need for reflection and reinvention of what is and is not acceptable conduct. This in turn saves time and effort that would otherwise be expended in repetitive instruction. These routines should be seen as the aspiration of all members of the school community whenever possible.

(p38)

▬ CHAPTER SUMMARY ▬

- Children's behaviour is highly complex and should be viewed as inseparable from academic achievement and all aspects of learning.

- Using the term 'behaviour' should be done with accuracy and precision, and in ways that can be properly understood by intended recipients, especially in written reports on children's development and learning.

- Teachers, through their own actions, are involved in a process whereby their pupils' development may be shaped through reinforcement of behaviours.

- Trainee teachers need to relate their knowledge and understanding of how behaviour shapes development to the standards required for UK Qualified Teaching Status (QTS).

▬ EXTENDED READING ▬

Ofsted (2013) *What About the Children? Joint Working between Adult and Children's Services When Parents or Carers Have Mental Ill Health and/or Drug and Alcohol Problems.* Manchester: Office for Standards in Education. A comprehensive and detailed look into childhood today and the impact of societal issues on children's behaviours and development, and therefore their learning.

7

ASSESSMENT AND DEVELOPMENT

WHY YOU SHOULD READ THIS CHAPTER

It is essential that trainee teachers learn the importance of assessing not only how groups of children perform in tests, but importantly how to assess what each child's capabilities are. Too many children fail to have their intellectual functioning properly assessed and recorded during the primary years, with the result that many experience years of underachievement and failure.

By the end of this chapter, you should know:

- what is meant by the term 'assessment';

- the importance of making accurate assessments of children's learning;

- how assessment needs to be informed through clear understanding of the individual and developmental needs of pupils;

- the importance of implementing effective and meaningful interventions to children appropriate to their levels of development; and

- how to relate assessment and intervention to the QTS standards.

INTRODUCTION

Too many schools have in the past failed to make accurate assessments of pupils' learning at different stages of their development, and too many teachers have attributed differing levels of development to lack of ability, poor motivation and lack of interest. The importance of teachers making accurate assessments of children's learning at different stages of their development and implementing appropriate, effective and purposeful interventions is now well recognised and is clearly embedded in the standards set out for Qualified Teaching Status (QTS) in the UK, as indicated in the following standards, where teachers should:

LINKS TO TEACHER STANDARDS

- *be aware of pupils' capabilities and prior knowledge, and plan teaching to build on these (A2);*
- *know when and how to differentiate appropriately (A5);*

(Continued)

(Continued)

- *have a clear understanding of the needs of all pupils (A5);*

- *know and understand how to assess the relevant subject and curriculum areas (A6);*

- *make use of formative and summative assessment to secure pupils' progress (A6); and*

- *use relevant data to monitor progress, set targets, and plan subsequent lessons (A6).*

(DfE, 2012)

EARLY ASSESSMENT IMPACTS HUGELY ON LATER DEVELOPMENT

It is crucial that accurate assessment takes place as early as possible, as it is during the early stages of development that important foundations for future learning are laid down. This is particularly so where children may have additional needs (DfE, 2015). If their developmental needs are not properly understood and addressed, children may then fail to have their learning needs accurately identified and assessed, with the result that they may go on to experience years of failure accompanied by a lowering of self-esteem and self-confidence (MacBlain, 2014; MacBlain et al., 2015). Early assessment is therefore crucial. Writing on the subject of children's development and learning, Hayward and Hayward (2016) have defined assessment as 'the process by which we discern the extent to which learning is taking place or has taken place' (p166). This is a most helpful definition because it poses what is perhaps a fundamental question for trainee teachers entering the profession: How do teachers know if a child has learned what they have asked of them? Indeed, Hayward and Hayward (2016) go on to qualify their definition by suggesting that when assessment is used properly, it also:

> *provides information about the starting point for what a young person might learn next – their next steps in learning. Next steps should build on what learners already know, say or are able to do, and should help them to grow both as people and learners.*

(p166)

ASSESSMENT: THE IMPORTANCE OF GETTING IT RIGHT

From the moment children enter educational settings, much of what they do is assessed and opinions about their abilities are formed by the adults around them. This, however, typically happens in a random and imprecise way, with descriptions of abilities often being shared among adults without proper evidence and often as anecdotes. It is not unusual, for example, to hear such comments as 'He's very quick for his age', 'He's a little slow with talking', 'She's very advanced for her age', 'She's a bright little thing', and so on. While such comments may have some degree of accuracy, they may also be largely wide of the mark, and even wholly inaccurate; typically, they will be based largely on assumptions and comparisons that adults have made with other children they have known or with some generalised notion they have of children's development. Here, one is reminded of one of our greatest thinkers, Einstein, who struggled with literacy until he was around 7 years of age (because of his dyslexia);

today, were he at primary school, he might have been placed on the school's special needs register as a child with low ability and learning difficulties.

APPROACHES TO ASSESSMENT

Approaches to assessment take two broad forms, formal and informal. With the former, assessment typically employs standardised tests and happens at a particular time and in a particular place; with the latter, assessment is typically continuous and informal. Every day, teachers engage in assessment of their pupils' learning, and they do this in a variety of ways, such as observation of pupils working on a range of tasks and activities, either by themselves or with others, and through questioning pupils. If done correctly, informal and continuous assessment can offer teachers very rich sources of information about how their pupils' levels of development are impacting on their learning; this is, however, often not the case with more formal methods of assessment such as standardised tests and even SATs.

— **CASE STUDY 7.1** ——————————————————————

An example of weak assessment and fuzzy thinking

Miss Welch teaches Kevin, who is 11 years of age and in his final year at primary school. She finds his behaviours very challenging and difficult to manage. His literacy and numeracy skills are very weak and well below those of her other pupils. She has just referred him to the school's educational psychologist. In her initial meeting with the educational psychologist, Miss Welch described Kevin as follows:

> I'm really worried about Kevin. He is still performing like the children in Key Stage 1. I like Kevin, and essentially he is really a good child, but his behaviour can be dreadful. He is really immature and acts like a 2-year-old at times. He continually disrupts the other children and he never really applies himself to improving reading and spelling, which are far worse than any of the other children in the class. His understanding of mathematics is probably the lowest of any of the children, though he does try to learn his times tables. I have tried everything possible to help him but without any success. None of my efforts seem to make any real difference. His concentration is almost non-existent, and he can't stick at anything for longer than a few minutes.

What becomes quickly apparent is that Miss Welch's description of Kevin tells the psychologist virtually nothing about Kevin's intellectual functioning and even less about his learning and patterns of behaviour. In truth, her account is dominated by vague and fuzzy statements, and really tells the psychologist more about her own frustrations and emotional reactions to Kevin's behaviour and lack of progress. Such phrases as 'I have tried everything possible to help him but without any success. None of my efforts seem to make any real difference' are vague, far too generalised and, perhaps most insightful, essentially emotive. Now, reflect upon the following case, where a different teacher, Miss Ford, who is in her first year working as a teacher, is also describing to the same educational psychologist a child named Leroy, also aged 11 years, who she has referred to the psychologist because of her concerns about his poor progress in literacy and numeracy and his poor concentration.

━ CASE STUDY 7.2 ━

Evidence-based thinking

Leroy is a very able child, and this is evident when one listens to him talking with the other children. He has a very good vocabulary and he is confident with initiating conversations with the other children when I ask the class to work in groups with each other. He appears to me to have difficulties with working memory, particularly his auditory sequential memory – I have noted how he has difficulties with recalling more than a few instructions that I have given, and he also struggles with memorising his multiplication times tables and with spellings – I can teach him something on Monday and he will have forgotten it by Wednesday. I have observed him working on a range of activities, and he gets very quickly distracted by what others around him are doing. He also processes visual information at a much slower rate than the other children – I note this each time he is being asked to copy written information from the whiteboard.

In the latter case, Miss Ford's account is precise and objective. She recounts her descriptions of Leroy by offering observations that are evidence-based, and therefore she is offering more accurate and valuable information about Leroy's learning to the educational psychologist.

TAKING TIME TO REFLECT PROPERLY ON THE LEARNING ENVIRONMENTS YOU CREATE

Assessment of children's learning, and especially aspects of learning that are problematic, must go far beyond exchanging vague anecdotes and descriptions that lack any real evidence base. Assessment should also properly consider the nature of the learning environments that teachers create, and importantly the match between how teachers teach and how their individual pupils learn. Failing to do so can lead to inaccurate identification of difficulties and erroneous assumptions that lead to ineffective interventions, which are at best of limited use and at worst useless (MacBlain, 2014; MacBlain et al., 2015).

━ KEY THEORY ━

Factors that make a difference to children's learning: the work of John Hattie

In a much-celebrated attempt to understand what constitutes effective teaching and learning in schools, Hattie (2008) set about synthesising findings from research spanning over a decade that involved the teaching and learning of literally thousands of children. Hattie examined a number of areas that, he proposed, play a major part in children's learning: the *children themselves*, their *homes* and *teachers*, their *schools*, the *curricula* they received, and the *teaching* and *learning approaches* that took place in their schools. Hattie suggested that a key factor in making a real difference to children's learning is the need for teachers to make their teaching and their pupils' learning 'visible'. By this, he meant teachers engaging in critical and reflective evaluation of their own teaching and actively seeking to view and understand learning through the eyes of the children they teach (Hattie, 2012; Hattie and Yates, 2014). Importantly, Hattie also suggested that the expectations teachers hold of their pupils and the perceptions they have of their abilities is crucial, and that these expectations and perceptions are based on what they believe their pupils can achieve (Hohnen and Murphy, 2016).

THE NEED FOR OBJECTIVITY

By being objective in their assessments, teachers free themselves from emotionally led and poorly formed perceptions of pupils' abilities that may have arisen from misinterpretations of ability that bear little relevance to their actual levels of development. By being objective, teachers can also better understand how their pupils approach learning tasks, meaning that they can engage more accurately in identification and assessment of individual needs, and more particularly how pupils approach new learning situations. To not do so may mean that the learning needs of children fail to be identified, meaning that they will then receive more of the same when what they have been doing is failing to meet their individual needs or, as Hattie (2008) has indicated:

> It is the case that we reinvent schooling every year. Despite any successes we may have had with this year's cohort of students, teachers have to start again next year with a new cohort. The greatest change that most students experience is the level of competence of the teacher ... It is surely easy to see how it is tempting for teachers to re-do the successes of the previous year, to judge students in terms of last year's cohort, and to insist on orderly progression through that which has worked before.

(p1)

Further insights into how teachers can engage objectively in the identification and assessment of their pupils can be found in the ideas of Marzano (Marzano, 2005, 2007; Marzano and Kendall, 2006). Marzano stressed how good teachers set clear goals, offer clear feedback and support pupils in how they interact with new learning; they set clear rules and insist on these being followed by all pupils. Importantly, good teachers establish and maintain relationships with their pupils that are positive and communicate to their pupils that they have high expectations of them. Through working in this way, teachers come to know their pupils much more fully; they also build their own pedagogical knowledge, which is then employed over and over in different situations and in different subject areas.

--- **KEY THEORY** --

Learning how to learn: an introduction to the ideas of Reuven Feuerstein

Now consider the work of Reuven Feuerstein (Feuerstein et al., 1980). Born in Botosani, Romania, in 1921, he began, after the Second World War, to work with child survivors of the Holocaust. When these children first arrived with Feuerstein, they were assessed using standardised IQ tests; Feuerstein noted, however, that they generally did not perform well on these tests. When he began working with them, he observed that they performed much better and their performances improved. This led him to examine more closely how they learned, and if, in fact, their ability was fixed, and, if not, then could it be developed, and could intellectual skills and abilities actually be changed in children's existing cognitive structures? This led him to develop the *concept* of 'dynamic assessment'. At the heart of Feuerstein's work is the idea that teachers should extend those processes that children employ when engaged in problem-solving and support them in managing their thinking through to the completion of tasks. Feuerstein suggested that teachers should act as 'mediators' and engage pupils in processes that extend their thinking to deeper levels. He maintained that the belief systems teachers hold about children's learning should view their potential as having almost

(Continued)

(Continued)

no limits, while also acknowledging the existence of artificial barriers that inhibit positive change. Feuerstein believed that every child can, with accurate identification and assessment and the appropriate interventions, become effective learners. By adopting such a belief system, teachers can, he argued, free themselves from the type of constrained thinking that might have limited them in the past and become more ambitious in what they believe is possible for every child. When teachers think and teach like this, a number of consequences occur within the thinking of the children they are teaching, which is, as Feuerstein termed, 'structural cognitive modifiability', or the idea that the cognitive structure of children's brains can become altered by an enabling process by which children learn how to learn. In effect, learning becomes cumulative, and this in turn impacts greatly on how they function throughout their lives (Burden, 1987). At the core of Feuerstein's notion of learning how to learn is what he referred to as 'mediated learning experience' (MLE), which is at the heart of his social interactionist theory of learning. Feuerstein et al. (1980) explained MLE as the way in which:

> stimuli emitted by the environment are transferred by a 'mediating' agent, usually a parent, sibling or other caregiver. This mediated agent, guided by his intentions, culture, and emotional investment, selects and organises the world of stimuli for the child ... Through this process of mediation, the cognitive structure of the child is affected.

(p16)

Core features of MLE are how teachers as mediators ensure their pupils have understood what is intended of them, explained why they are asking their pupils to work on particular tasks, and that the activities their pupils will be working on are understood by them and they understand how the activities have value beyond the immediate task they are engaging in and can lead to additional generalisation of their existing knowledge (Figure 7.1). In this way, teachers can engage in accurate identification and assessment of pupils' learning, establish effective learning environments and support pupils in realising their potential.

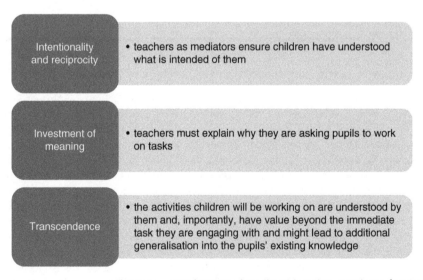

Figure 7.1 Core features of mediated learning experience (Burden, 1987)

■■ ACTIVITY ■■

View the following YouTube video: *The Art & Science of Teaching - Dr Robert Marzano* (**www.youtube. com/watch?v=YhB_R_FT9y4**), which introduces Marzano's ideas on teaching and learning and how teachers might maximise their impact on their pupils' learning. Then consider your own experiences of children's learning. What sort of questions did you ask that had the greatest impact upon the children's learning?

HOW SHOULD WE VIEW INTELLECTUAL DEVELOPMENT?

Without question, one of the most controversial areas in the psychology of human development is that of 'intelligence'. Theorists and philosophers have argued for centuries about the nature of intelligence – what it is and, perhaps most controversially of all, whether or not it is inherited and if it can be measured (MacBlain, 2014, p136). In her introductory text to the study of psychology, Hayes (1994) offered the following cautionary note to students:

Intelligence is probably the single most controversial topic in psychology. People hold widely different opinions on what it is, how it develops and how relevant it is for living; and these differences have sometimes developed into highly acrimonious debates. One of the main reasons for this is political: intelligence is not just an academic issue … The political implications of intelligence theory centre on three issues: social stratification, education and eugenics.

(p178)

Hayes (1994) also proposed that it was when the Western world moved towards a meritocratic system, where status was accorded to those who were considered to be more intellectually able, that the *concept* of intelligence 'first emerged' (p179). She also emphasised how theories that sought to explain the nature of intelligence were very influential in directing the course of practice that took place within schools over the last two centuries. Around the same time, Gross also offered students of psychology the following definition of intelligence by Wechsler (1944), who explained intelligence as 'The aggregate of the global capacity to act purposefully, think rationally, to deal effectively with the environment' (cited in Gross, 1992, p840); this consideration of the nature of intelligence still informs thinking today.

SEEING INTELLECTUAL DEVELOPMENT DIFFERENTLY

Some years ago, Gardner (1983) offered what was then a new and different way of thinking about children's intellectual development and what was then generally understood as 'intelligence'. He proposed that intelligence is made up of the following 'multiple intelligences' that are systems in their own right but that interact with one another: *linguistic, logical-mathematical, spatial, musical, bodily-kinaesthetic, interpersonal* and *intrapersonal*; more recently, he has even surmised that there may be others, such as *naturalist intelligence*, that could be added to his original list. Gardner's theory of 'multiple intelligences' has, however, been criticised by some on the grounds that it is not possible to empirically verify elements of his theory, and therefore it is open to question. Brooks et al. (2004) have, for example, suggested that it is lacking in testability, resulting from 'an ambiguity of the theory, in that it is not clear to what extent the intelligences are supposed to operate separately or interconnectedly' (p55). This said, his notion of 'multiple intelligences' has become very popular with many teachers as they use the *concept* to celebrate different aspects of children's development.

ACTIVITY

View the following two YouTube videos: *Feuerstein Method* (**www.youtube.com/watch?v=dSG EMrOKHVI**) and *Down Syndrome Film 'Looking Up On Down'* (*Glow Films/Feuerstein Institute Film by David Goodwin*) (**www.youtube.com/watch?v=IqSQI6VJgLk**). Then consider how children's learning can be negatively impacted by artificial barriers and how these barriers might be avoided by teachers.

DEVELOPMENT AND ADDITIONAL NEEDS

Trainee teachers will quickly become aware of the significant numbers of children now in mainstream schools who have additional needs. Some are born with particular conditions and others develop difficulties as they grow. Less than a decade ago, Laura Clark, an educational correspondent writing for the UK national newspaper the *Daily Mail* on 13 July 2012, commented as follows:

> *Children as young as one are being labelled as having special educational needs by their nurseries ... By the age of five, more than one in six children – 173,525 – has been diagnosed as having special needs ... Most are diagnosed during their first year at school ... Figures released yesterday by the Department for Education showed that 19.8 per cent of children across the school system – more than 1.6 million – have been given the label.*

(Clark, 2012, p12)

The reporting of statistics such as these in a popular newspaper is worrying and presents a stark picture. Even more worrying perhaps is the following, again offered by Clark (2012):

> *Ofsted revealed two years ago that schools may have wrongly labelled as many as 450,000 children as having special needs ... the Government's former adviser on speech and language, warned that this was often 'used as an explanation for failure'.*

(p12)

Some months previously, the journalist Peter Stanford, writing in another UK national paper, the *Daily Telegraph*, offered the following:

> *Many experts fear that funds earmarked to help children with learning difficulties are being redirected to cope with a new tide of social deprivation that is washing up in the classroom. Children from troubled homes, who turn up at schools with behavioural problems, are being routinely put on the SEN register alongside those with more specific learning difficulties, such as dyslexia and dyspraxia.*

(Stanford, 2012, p23)

In 2009, the Office for Standards in Education (Ofsted) undertook a major review of special educational needs and disability in England (Ofsted, 2010) in which they highlighted the fact that the term 'special educational needs' was being too widely used. Approximately 50 per cent of the schools and early years providers they visited employed the *concepts* of 'low attainment' and 'relatively slow progress' as the chief indicators for deciding whether a child had a special educational need. The inspectors reported on schools they had visited who identified children as having special educational needs when in fact their needs were not significantly different to most of the other children. The report concluded that while these children were underachieving, this was in part due to the provision offered by schools being 'not good enough', with expectations of these children being 'too low'. The report also concluded that in some instances, children were being incorrectly identified as having special educational needs, and that some provision that was additional and that required additional funding was being used 'to make up for day-to-day teaching and pastoral support'. The report also highlighted the fact that:

> In the case of children and young people who need complex and specialist support from health and other services to enable them to thrive and develop, the term 'educational needs' does not always accurately reflect their situation. Both these considerations suggest that we should not only move away from the current system of categorisation of needs but also start to think critically about the way terms are used.

> (Ofsted, 2010, p9)

The report also identified a number of key elements that underpinned successful learning for children and young people as follows:

- *they looked to the teacher for their main learning and to the support staff for support;*

- *assessment was secure, continuous and acted upon;*

- *teachers planned opportunities for pupils to collaborate, work things out for themselves and apply what they had learnt to different situations;*

- *teachers' subject knowledge was good, as was their understanding of pupils' needs and how to help them;*

- *lesson structures were clear and familiar but allowed for adaptation and flexibility;*

- *all aspects of a lesson were well thought out and any adaptations needed were made without fuss to ensure that everyone in class had access;*

- *teachers presented information in different ways to ensure all children and young people understood;*

- *teachers adjusted the pace of the lesson to reflect how children and young people were learning;*

- *the staff understood clearly the difference between ensuring that children and young people were learning and keeping them occupied;*

- *respect for individuals was reflected in high expectations for their achievement; and*

- *the effectiveness of specific types of support was understood and the right support was put in place at the right time.*

> (Ofsted, 2010, p47)

DYSPRAXIA: A CASE IN POINT

One example of how developmental difficulties impact on children with additional needs can be located within the condition dyspraxia. The following case study illustrates the types of difficulties that many children with this condition experience on a daily basis in school.

━ CASE STUDY 7.3 ━

Making the correct assessment

Jenny is 9 years of age and has just started in Key Stage 2. Her previous teacher described Jenny as 'a lovely girl who is very bright but struggles to keep up with the other children, hopelessly disorganised and very easily distracted, even by the slightest noise, she almost never finishes written work on time'. Her previous teacher has expressed particular concerns about the nature of Jenny's handwriting, which she has indicated is 'almost always illegible'. She has also been concerned by Jenny's progress in PE lessons, describing her as 'having real problems following rules and being in the wrong place at the wrong time'. Ever since starting school, Jenny has been observed by her different teachers and classroom assistants to be very clumsy and overly sensitive and as being very quick to get upset and cry. Her parents have reported that she has only just managed to ride a two-wheel bicycle without stabilisers at 9 years of age and reported how tying her shoelaces still presents Jenny with significant problems. Jenny's reading and spelling continue to present her with significant challenges, and now at age 9 years and 2 months she has only scored a recent reading age of 7 years and 6 months; her literacy skills are delayed and do not seem to match her above-average intellectual abilities.

Jenny has the condition known as dyspraxia, and is typical of a number of children who present with difficulties in their primary years of schooling. A particular problem for Jenny lies in the fact that the difficulties she has presented with since starting school have not been well understood by her teachers. Addressing how we understand this complex condition of dyspraxia, Boon (2010) commented as follows:

> If you ask different professionals what dyspraxia is, you get different answers, depending on their field of expertise ... The Dyspraxia Foundation ... defines dyspraxia as 'an impairment or immaturity of the organization of movement. Associated with this there may be problems of language, perception and thought.' It is fundamentally an immaturity in the way that the brain processes information, which results in messages not being properly or fully transmitted to the body.

(p7)

The Dyspraxia Foundation has suggested that dyspraxia affects up to 10 per cent of the general population and that some 2 per cent are affected severely. The Foundation also suggests that males are more affected than females and that statistically it is likely that in a class of 30 children, there is likely to be one child with dyspraxia (MacBlain, 2014, p185). To gain a better understanding of dyspraxia and the related condition of *developmental coordination disorder* and how it impacts on children, we can look more closely at 'movement', and particularly the relationship between movement and the brain. Movement is involved in almost every activity that children engage in. While for most children activities such as running and jumping, writing and drawing, and speaking develop in a relatively straightforward way, for children with dyspraxia this is often not the case, and these activities can present them with significant problems. Take, for example, the case of language development in young children. When muscles in the mouth or throat of a child are affected in some way, then speech and even general language processing can be compromised with some children experiencing difficulties with articulating words and phrases; in more severe cases, this may cause their speech to be incomprehensible (Macintyre, 2002).

UNDERSTANDING THE IMPORTANCE OF MOVEMENT

Movement is also very important in developing children's self-esteem. A child's poor self-esteem may result from problems such as not being able to ride a two-wheel bicycle without stabilisers until much older, poor ball control, and the unwillingness of peers to choose them for their games. In school, teachers may observe very poor handwriting and presentation of written work, problems with organisation, difficulties learning to tell the time and repeat times tables with accuracy, and so on. Teachers need to understand, therefore, that such difficulties are not a manifestation of low ability, but rather an indication of a child's dyspraxia. They may also experience difficulties sitting at a table for even short periods of time and may be observed to move about a lot, and even squirm in their seats. Physical education can be particularly challenging for children with dyspraxia as their immaturities with motor coordination can mean that they struggle to keep up with other children; throwing and catching can be particularly problematic for children with dyspraxia.

UNDERSTANDING THE IMPORTANCE OF PLANNING

A further way in which children with dyspraxia can be affected is with their planning of thoughts and actions. They may, for example, present with problems in planning their ideas for a written story. It has been my (the author) experience in the past when working as an educational psychologist that children with dyspraxia were often referred for assessment around 9 years of age when their teachers were expecting them to write longer stories in contrast to previously, when their teachers had asked them to write only sentences to match pictures. Children with dyspraxia can also be very easily distracted by what is happening around them (e.g. by noises in the classroom and visual stimuli, and even by their own thoughts); this may often lead to them not finishing their work on time. This should not be seen by teachers as poor concentration or poor attitude, but as a manifestation of their condition.

━━ **KEY THEORY** ━━━━━━━━━━━━━━━━━━━━━━━━━━━━━━━━

The functioning of the brain and the growth of brain cells

Macintyre and McVitty (2004) have explained how brain cells:

> work together to receive, analyse and act on information from both external, i.e. environmental sources, and internal feelings, i.e. pain, hunger and the different emotions. As different experiences occur, these neurons join into networks that work together as systems to facilitate specific functions such as vision or hearing, movement or paying attention.

(pp5-6)

(Continued)

(Continued)

They go on to explain how each neuron in the brain:

> has an axon, a long spindle that leads to branching dendrites. These connect to other dendrites over a synapse, i.e. a gap, to approximately one hundred thousand other neurons. Chemicals such as dopamine act as neurotransmitters, passing messages from one cell to the next. The vast number of cells and connections mean that an infinite number of connections can be made and unmade.

(pp5-6)

As children grow, their brains develop, and this forms the basis for learning. Every part of the body is connected in some form with the brain, and some parts have more neurons than others; this explains why some parts of the body are more sensitive than others and more receptive to touch and to pain. In children with dyspraxia, this process is different, in that it is characterised by immaturity (MacBlain, 2014).

ADVANCED DEVELOPMENT: GIFTED AND TALENTED LEARNERS

There are many children who are born with unique 'gifts' and the potential to achieve at the highest levels. Developmentally, such children appear to be way ahead of their peers, often learning to walk and talk at an early age, access literacy and numeracy with apparent ease, demonstrate abilities to play musical instruments competently in their first years, and display wonderful talents in art and drawing. While these children typically find learning in school during their first years to be very easy, they can also present challenges; some may find the school curriculum too easy and become bored.

━━ CASE STUDY 7.4 ━━━━━━━━━━━━━━━━━━━━━━━━━━━━━━━━━

Recognising and matching ability to development

David is 4 years of age and is due to complete his last year at nursery school. His parents have been very aware since he was only a few months old that he is very advanced for his age and they are concerned that his needs will not be properly met when he attends primary school. They have referred him to an educational psychologist for a private assessment. They are especially concerned that he will not be properly recognised as being extremely able. In their initial discussions with the educational psychologist, David's parents describe him as 'extremely able and very advanced for his age ... he was talking after only 6 months, and at 2 years of age could read books ... always active and curious about everything'. When the educational psychologist meets with David at his home, she observes him as he is engaged in some activities, talks with his parents, and invites David to work on some subtests from the Wechsler Preschool and Primary Scale of Intelligence (WPPSI); his scores indicate that he is a highly intelligent child in the superior range of functioning.

David is clearly a very able child of above-average intellectual ability. It is also clear that his very high levels of intellectual ability and his advanced cognitive development have not been fully understood and recognised by his teachers. Though relatively few in number, there will be children in primary schools who, like David, are very advanced in their intellectual ability; there will also be others who have advanced natural abilities in art, music, sport and physicality, and who may be considered as being gifted in comparison to most of their peers. Some years ago, the Good Schools Guide (2013a) offered the following comments:

> Gifted is one of a number of issues in education that cause the blood to stir. For some 'Gifted' is an elitist concept that beggars definition ... In England, the Department for Education ... distinguishes between gifted learners and talented children ... Gifted learners are those who have particular abilities in one or more curriculum subjects ... Talented learners are those who have particular abilities in the creative arts (such as music, art and design, drama, dance) and PE. Some schools (and parents) prefer the term 'more able' or 'high ability' ... but the term 'gifted' is very much part of the official language.

The Good Schools Guide (2013b) also commented:

> Exceptionally bright children often show good hand–eye co-ordination, though sometimes their handwriting lags behind their reading and other skills. Some children may refuse to produce any work on paper because of the frustration caused when they are unable to live up to their own impossibly high standards in handwriting and drawing.

Addressing the complex notion of assessing children thought to be exceptionally able and/or talented, the Good Schools Guide (2013b) offered the following:

> Others are particularly skillful in playing with ideas, in using their imagination and in being creative. Such characteristics do not always show up on traditional intelligence tests but parents who suspect their child may be gifted should not be afraid to talk things over with the teachers at school.

This Guide has drawn attention to some of the challenges that face children who are very advanced in aspects of their ability and potential; for example, the all-too-frequent lack of a positive perception of what it is to be extremely able or talented, and an apparent unwillingness by such children to demonstrate their exceptionally high levels of ability in front of peers for fear of embarrassment and even of being bullied. Further challenges faced by these children may include an absence of proper assessment and testing and appropriate intervention. Indeed, some special educational needs, such as dyslexia and dyspraxia, that might mask the underlying cognitive abilities and advanced intellectual ability in very able children may be masked by their early problems with reading and spelling, resulting in a mismatch between academic attainment and verbal and emotional ability. Often the results of such mismatches can present as frustration, increased disaffection and even poor behaviour (MacBlain, 2014; MacBlain et al., 2015).

Of concern is the fact that less than a decade ago, Ofsted (2013a, pp8–10) published a report that presented some very challenging findings and observations for teachers of more able children, some of which are especially relevant to practice in primary schools (Figure 7.2).

> • ... Transition arrangements from primary to secondary school are not effective enough to ensure that students maintain their academic momentum into Year 7.
>
> • ... Many students become used to performing at a lower level than they are capable of.
>
> • ... The curriculum and the quality of homework required improvement.

Figure 7.2   Findings from Ofsted (2013a)

The implications of this report are substantial and pose a number of questions. How, for example, will primary schools determine who is more able and who is not? Will primary schools give greater credence to attainment as opposed to intellectual abilities that have been masked in the course of development by conditions such as dyslexia and dyspraxia? Will secondary schools assume that children coming to them from primary schools who have demonstrated higher attainments be the most able and put them in higher 'sets' where children are more motivated to succeed academically? Take the example of Rashid and Rory below.

━━ CASE STUDY 7.5 ━━━

Accuracy of assessment

Rashid was born into a family where both parents are highly educated and have professional careers. Since starting primary school, Rashid's parents realised that he was not as intellectually able as many of their friends' children of the same age and most other children in his class. Addressing this situation, they arranged for Rashid to have private tutoring in literacy and maths and spend a great deal of time taking him to museums and galleries to widen his education; they have many books in their home and take a great deal of time going through these books with Rashid. In contrast, Rory is an exceptionally able and very advanced child in many areas; from his first years, he was physically very coordinated and could play football very well, had a very strong memory, and processed information and solved problems very quickly. Reading and mathematics seemed to be very easy for him, and at 3 years of age he was able to read short books with ease and write many words. Since starting primary school, however, he presented with significant behaviour problems. When he was 2 years of age, his father left home, which affected him deeply, and since then he has been reared by his mother, who sadly was diagnosed with depression and anxiety shortly after Rory's father left. His mother spends most of her time alone in her bedroom and does not communicate much with Rory. Now in his final year of primary school, Rory is described by his teachers as a 'problem child' who has a very poor concentration span and who is mostly unwilling to try to learn. When young, he found schoolwork boring and unstimulating and too easy for him.

Now, however, he is perceived by his teachers to lack ability and has acquired poor literacy and numeracy skills, in contrast to Rashid, who has been privately tutored and supported by his parents. Both children are now preparing to transition to secondary school with descriptions that are inaccurate and that do not reflect their true levels of ability and potential.

CHAPTER SUMMARY

- It is essential that trainee teachers understand the importance of assessing each child's capabilities.

- Too many children are failed by not having their true abilities and capabilities properly assessed, with the result that they go on to experience underachievement and failure.

- Trainee teachers need to understand the importance of making accurate assessments of children's learning and know how assessment can inform them of the individual and developmental needs of their pupils.

- Proper assessment facilitates the implementation of effective and meaningful interventions for children, so that expectations of their progress in learning are matched to their levels of development.

- Trainee teachers need to understand how assessment and intervention relates to the required standards for UK Qualified Teaching Status (QTS).

EXTENDED READING

Macintyre, C. and McVitty, K. (2004) *Movement and Learning in the Early Years: Supporting Dyspraxia (DCD) and Other Difficulties*. London: Paul Chapman. A beautifully written book that looks at movement in young children and explains with great sensitivity the condition of dyspraxia. This text would go a long way in helping trainee teachers to understand the nature of holistic development in children.

8

FUTURE CHALLENGES

WHY YOU SHOULD READ THIS CHAPTER

How children develop today is vastly different to that of previous generations, and even decades. This process is accelerating, and teachers working with future generations of children will be dealing with issues that perhaps have not yet been thought of. Trainee teachers, therefore, will not only need to continue adapting their skills and increasing their knowledge about factors affecting children's development, but importantly will need to understand that they themselves are also part of an emerging and rapidly changing global dynamic.

By the end of this chapter, you should know:

- how a rapidly changing world is impacting on children's development, and therefore their learning;

- that trainee teachers have to prepare themselves to work effectively with children and families from diverse cultural backgrounds;

- how factors such as nutrition and obesity, over-sexualisation, poverty, and technology are impacting on and shaping children's development; and

- how to relate emerging challenges that are impacting on children's development to the requirement of the QTS standards.

INTRODUCTION

Children's development is grounded in the historical cultures and societies they are born into, the communities in which they grow up, and increasingly the ever-changing and globalised world around them; every one of these elements impacts in different ways on children's development and, of course, their learning. Recently, Arnott (2016) commented on how all of us now 'live in a socio-cultural world where our knowledge, beliefs and learning are shaped by experience and culture' (p331). Arnott further emphasised how 'future childhood experience will always be different from the generation before' (p332). Trainee teachers, therefore, will need to fully appreciate how the children they teach in the future will have vastly different experiences to those of today and that the nature of many of these experiences are as yet unknown.

A defining characteristic of many schools in the UK over recent decades that has impacted greatly on the training of teachers has been the considerable increase in diversity, evidenced by the number of children with complex special needs who are now taught in mainstream as opposed to special schools and the rise in numbers of children whose first language is not English (MacBlain and Purdy, 2010; MacBlain et al., 2017). Back in 2012, the National Association for Language Development in the Curriculum (NALDIC, 2012), for example, reported on the annual school census of that year, which showed how one in six pupils in primary schools in England did not have English as their first language. In the same year, NALDIC reported that over 3 million children between the ages of 5 and 16 in UK schools were speaking in excess of 360 languages between them. A further characteristic of the increasing rate of change in UK schools has been the sustained growth in the use of digital technology by children. The role that teachers need to play in supporting children as such new challenges emerge is clearly embedded in the standards set out for Qualified Teaching Status (QTS) in the UK, as indicated in the following standards, where teachers should:

■ LINKS TO TEACHER STANDARDS

- *set goals that stretch and challenge pupils of all backgrounds, abilities and dispositions (A1);*

- *demonstrate an awareness of the physical, social and intellectual development of children, and know how to adapt teaching to support pupils' education at different stages of development (A5);*

- *have a clear understanding of the needs of all pupils, including those with special educational needs; those of high ability; those with English as an additional language; those with disabilities; and be able to use and evaluate distinctive teaching approaches to engage and support them (A5); and*

- *communicate effectively with parents with regard to pupils' achievements and well-being (A8).*

(DfE, 2012)

TOMORROW'S CHILDREN

How children develop in the next decades will present significant challenges for today's trainee teachers. Examples of challenges that have arisen in recent years and that signify future challenges can be seen in the following three extracts. The first of these was proposed less than a decade ago by McDowall Clark (2010), who offered a stark indication of how childhood is becoming more regulated when he highlighted the changing nature of children's play:

> *Children do not play out in the street anymore, they are rarely allowed to travel to school on their own … Children spend an increasing proportion of their time in specially designated places such as day nurseries, out-of-school clubs and their own bedrooms, frequently fitted out with the latest technology. Childhood is progressively more regulated so that instead of being a natural part of public life, it takes place in private.*

(p1)

A hard-hitting report around the same time, *Removing Barriers to Literacy*, published by Ofsted (2011), drew attention to what has become a worrying trend in children's development when they highlighted the increased frequency of young children entering primary school with delayed language development and emotional disturbance:

Of the barriers facing the youngest children … a common problem was some form of delay of their development in speech and language. In one nursery visited, for example, where almost all children were of White British origin, approximately 30 per cent of the three-year-olds started nursery with a marked speech delay. Another common problem that placed children at early disadvantage was a disturbed start to their lives. In one nursery visited, most of the two-year-olds had already had some form of social care intervention by the time they joined the nursery.

(p14)

In 2012, Graeme Paton, then education editor for the national online UK newspaper *The Telegraph*, drew attention to concerns raised by a number of 'experts', as follows:

In a letter to The Daily Telegraph, academics and authors said that controversial education reforms are robbing under-fives of the ability to play and leading to the 'schoolification' of the early years … today's letter … warned of 'widespread concern about the direction of the current revision' … The experts … suggested the system was 'too inflexible to cater for the highly diverse developmental needs of young children'.

(Paton, 2012)

The above extracts point to a changing world where aspects of children's development are evolving at what some might consider to be an astonishing pace, driven by factors such as the rapid growth in technology, increased materialism, globalisation, poverty, and an almost overwhelming influence of social media on the lives of young people, the effects of which are as yet barely understood.

Figure 8.1   Challenges facing trainee teachers in the future

THE EMERGENCE OF THE DIGITAL CHILD

In her exploration of the inevitable change that digital technology is bringing about in children's development, Arnott (2016) has emphasised how 'perceptions of childhood have become polarised' (p331), and she goes further by drawing attention to how, in this respect, we are now:

> seeing divergent discourses emerging with those fearful of technologies perpetuating the child-at-risk discourse and those excited by technologies embracing the empowering capabilities that technologies can offer (Craft, 2012). That is to say that adults are either viewing children as passive and in need of protection, or active and capable of deciphering messages in media and learning from them (Marsh, 2004).
>
> (p331)

While practising primary teachers acknowledge concerns about the extent of technology in the lives of their pupils, they also acknowledge its benefits. Recently, MacBlain et al. (2017) alluded to some of the concerns felt by teachers and parents when they highlighted the increased amount of screen time engaged in by children:

> In a recent survey of more than 1000 parents, it is reported that time spent watching TV by children under 5 has increased from 2.4 to 2.6 hours per day over the past year, and that 73 per cent of under-5s are using a tablet or computer compared to 23 per cent in 2012. Children are using tablets or computers by the age of 2 and when they reach 6 more than 40 per cent are using them every day (CHILDWISE, 2015).
>
> (p168)

MacBlain et al. (2017, p168) went on to indicate how children between the ages of 8 and 11 are spending increased time per week online, '10.5 hours in 2014 vs 9.2 hours in 2013' (Ofcom, 2014). They also cited the example of a recent UK report, which explored play and creativity in preschool children's use of apps, that indicated how some 65 per cent of children between the ages of 3 and 7 have access to a tablet computer, with parents reporting how children under 5 years of age 'use tablets for an average of 1 hour and 19 minutes on a typical weekday (Marsh et al., 2015)'.

ACTIVITY

View the following YouTube video: *Psychology Lecture: Child Development in the Digital Age* (**www. youtube.com/watch?v=8rTnfCrwloY**). Then consider how children influence the behaviour of their parents in order to access digital media.

DEVELOPMENT IN A GLOBAL CONTEXT

Today's children are growing up in a world that is becoming increasingly interconnected. It is not uncommon now for teachers in the UK to find themselves teaching children from other parts of the world who grow up in homes and communities characterised by different and very diverse cultural heritages. Indeed, the cultural make-up in many schools across the UK has changed significantly in past decades with 'new arrivals' entering the education system. This has increased in more recent years as large numbers of families fleeing conflict in other parts of the world have arrived in the UK. Just over a decade ago, Hicks (2004) commented as follows:

> We can only understand life today in our own communities if it is set in the wider global context. What happens elsewhere in the world constantly impacts on our daily lives even if we may not have been aware of it ... Climate change, energy use, economic growth, wealth and poverty, and violent conflict affect our local communities and day-to-day living ... The forces of globalization, engineered by the rich world, are binding the world more closely together, but are also being more fiercely resisted than ever before.

(p19)

More recently, Green and Kerr (2019) pointed towards the impact that globalisation is having on schools in the UK through having to adhere to international standards and a changing ideology that places economic well-being at the centre of education, as opposed to nurturing individuality and creativity in children:

> The movement towards 'educational multilateralism' (Mundy, 1998), where the setting of 'standards' has moved beyond the national to the global level, further changes the expectations placed upon schools, education being linked to the development of 'human capital' and the knowledge economy. Thus, representing a further ideological shift in defining the purpose of education, the role of schools and economic well-being.

(p191)

CHILDREN'S HEALTH AND DEVELOPMENT

It is now accepted that diet and nutrition play an enormous part in children's development, with deficiencies in these areas often presenting unseen challenges for young children's learning, with consequences then for those teachers tasked with managing their learning. Siberfield (2016) recently encapsulated this area of concern when she drew attention to how, despite apparent 'increased prosperity', the health and well-being of children across the UK is giving rise for concern; in doing so, she offered the following very worrying statistics:

> During the past 25 years ... the health of children in the UK is considered to be much poorer than children in other comparable European Countries ... with, for example, an estimated 2,000 more children dying per year in the UK than Sweden ... During the past 15 years, experts in child health and research have consistently argued that this gap will continue to widen unless the causes of poverty are properly addressed.

(p283)

NUTRITION

Good nutrition is extremely important not only for children's physical development, but also for their cognitive development, and therefore their learning. Buckler and Castle (2014) have emphasised how without proper nutrition, 'the human body will not develop in a way that its genes would wish', and importantly that 'inadequate nutrition has implications for brain development' (p84). They have also made the following quite worrying assertion that 'few people stop to consider that healthy eating is equally important in helping our children's brains achieve their functional potential' (p84). Not only are a lack of food and starvation detrimental to children's physical development and their learning and well-being, but so is overeating the wrong type of food, which can lead to obesity even in very young children.

OBESITY

The problem of obesity, which Buckler and Castle (2014) have described as 'virulent, especially in Western societies' (p84), has now been recognised as a significant and disturbing aspect of development in children. Obesity contributes to issues of general health and even mental health, as well as children's well-being, with the latter often related directly to children's perceptions of their self-image; the extent of the problem is worrying. The number of overweight children under 5 years of age has, for example, increased across the globe from 32 million in 1990 to 42 million in 2013, with an increase of 4 million to 9 million overweight or obese children being reported by the World Health Organization (WHO) African region during this same period (WHO, 2015). A further worrying trend is reflected in the fact that the majority of children who are obese are now growing up in developing countries, with an estimated rate of increase being 30 per cent greater than in developed countries. The WHO has also estimated that if this trend continues, the number of overweight or obese infants and young children globally will increase over future years to some 70 million in 2025.

Recently, the Health and Social Care Information Centre (HSCIC, 2015) drew attention to the fact that in England, the number of children aged 4 to 5 years in 2013/14 who were obese was around 9.5 per cent. The HSCIC also indicated the proportion of obese children in England aged 10 to 11 in 2013/14 was around 19.1 per cent, which was an increase from the previous year at 18.9 per cent and higher than 2006/07 at 17.5 per cent (Table 8.1). More recently, in January 2016, the Commission on Ending Childhood Obesity (WHO, 2016) presented its final report to the WHO, making key recommendations to governments across the globe, aimed at reversing the worrying trend of obesity in children below the age of 5 years.

Table 8.1   Proportion of obese children in England

Age	Year	Per cent
4-5	2013/14	9.5
10-11	2006/07	17.5
10-11	2012/13	18.9
10-11	2013/14	19.1

Source: HSCIC (2015)

IS CHILDREN'S DEVELOPMENT BEING OVER-SEXUALISED?

A growing concern among many teachers and parents, as well as other professionals, has been the increased sexual activity among younger children; this is not just a UK issue, but a global one (MacBlain et al., 2017). Just over a decade ago, in one of their reports, *World Health Report: Reducing*

Risks, Promoting Health Life (WHO, 2002), the World Health Organization drew attention to the importance of 'sexual health' in children; the report emphasised how the *concept* of 'health' should go beyond simply looking at physical factors, but crucially should also address factors relating to the associated emotional and social development of children:

> *Sexual health is a state of physical, emotional, mental and social well-being related to sexuality; it is not the absence of disease, dysfunction or infirmity ... For sexual health to be attained and maintained, the sexual rights of all persons must be respected, protected and fulfilled.*

Currie et al. (2008), cited in Cowie (2012, p145), reported just over a decade ago on how young people within the UK are becoming more sexually active at a younger age, and more specifically that over 30 per cent of children in a study they undertook reported having sex by 16 years of age, with this trend having increased since the 1960s. They concluded that young people were experimenting more with sex and showed fewer inhibitions than young people in previous generations. Cowie also commented on how body piercing and tattoos had become a means by which young people choose to demonstrate that they have moved beyond adolescence and into adulthood. Cowie (2012) has gone further, emphasising the emergence of 'new' behaviours in children and young people that characterise this move beyond adolescence as follows:

> *The proof can be circulating intimate pictures of, for example, genital or belly button piercing, on the internet or by mobile phone ... They will often rely more on blogs and informal chat with one another in order to seek clarification about sexual behaviour.*

> (p145)

A further and concerning study cited by Cowie, which was undertaken by Moore and Rosenthal (2006), indicated how 'young people are engaging in a wide range of sexual behaviours, including solo sex, anal and oral sex' (Cowie, 2012, p145). A report commissioned by the Department for Children, *Letting Children Be Children: Report of an Independent Review of the Commercialization and Sexualization of Childhood* (Bailey, 2011), has drawn attention to the pressures on children today to grow up too quickly, which take:

> *different but related forms: the pressure to take part in a sexualized life before they are ready to do so; and the commercial pressure to consume the vast range of goods and services that are available to children and young people of all ages.*

> (p6)

A further worrying report by the NSPCC, *How Safe Are Our Children? The Most Comprehensive Overview of Child Protection in the UK* (Jütte et al., 2015), indicated how in the UK, police recorded some 36,500 sexual offences against children in 2013–2014. More recently, Elizabeth Rigby, the media editor for the popular UK newspaper *The Times*, drew attention to how the 'sexting epidemic' in Britain is a 'time-bomb' (Rigby, 2016, p13). In the same newspaper, reporters Rachel Sylvester and Alice Thompson quoted the chief constable of Norfolk, who offered the following worrying statistics, suggesting aspects of young people's development that appear to be largely beyond the control of adults:

In the late 1990s there were only 7,000 indecent images of children in circulation in Britain. Now, conservatively, I would say that there are 100 million ... There has been an 80 per cent increase in cases in the last three years, with police carrying out 70,000 child sexual abuse investigations last year.

(Sylvester and Thompson, 2016, p12)

THE INFLUENCE OF MEDIA AND MATERIALISM ON DEVELOPMENT

It is now recognised that today's children are born into increasingly modernised and institutionalised societies in which key aspects of their development are being shaped by extreme levels of materialism, which leads to many children growing up too quickly (Elkind, 1981). Indeed, Cregan and Cuthbert (2014) have pointed towards an 'impending crisis for children and childhood' in what they view as the Global North of the world, and they have suggested that this 'impending crisis' has been spreading through rapidly developing countries such as Malaysia (p52). Drawing upon the work of Niner et al. (2013), they have likened the growing influence of modernisation on young people in Malaysia to a '"social tsunami", which apocalyptically threatens to sweep away everything in its path'.

Cregan and Cuthbert (2014) have been more explicit in their concerns regarding the impact of materialism in those more affluent and developed countries across the globe:

another set of apprehensions arises from the conditions of material affluence ... These include anxiety about the impact of technology on the lives of children; the precocious sexualization of children through age-inappropriate clothing, popular clothing and merchandise; the progressive sequestering and inactivity of children inside their home due to fears of dangers outside the home; and children's preoccupation with technologized entertainment.

(p50)

Cregan and Cuthbert's concerns are very relevant to why teachers now entering the profession need to inform themselves as to how materialism is affecting children's development, and therefore their learning. They emphasise how anxiety about technology is impacting on the lives of children, with many parents now finding themselves under pressure from their children to respond to requests and demands to buy expensive technological devices. Trainee teachers who have been on placement in schools will, for example, be aware of the number of even very young children who either own mobile phones or have been requesting these from their parents. Some years before Cregan and Cuthbert wrote the above, the UK newspaper the *Daily Telegraph* published a letter in 2006, signed by over 100 teachers, psychologists and other experts, calling on the government to 'prevent the death of childhood':

Since children's brains are still developing, they cannot adjust – as full-grown adults can – to the effects of ever more rapid technological and cultural change. They still need what developing human beings have always needed, including real food (as opposed to processed 'junk'), real play (as opposed to sedentary, screen-based entertainment), first-hand experience of the world they live in and regular interaction with the real-life significant adults in their lives.

(Fenton, 2006, p1)

HUMAN CONFLICT: ITS IMPACT ON CHILDREN'S DEVELOPMENT

We all live in a world that is increasingly becoming globalised; children born in countries on the other side of the globe can find themselves suddenly having to leave their country of birth and move to another country such as the UK. There are many examples of children such as this who are being taught in schools in the UK today, and it is not unheard of for teachers to find themselves managing the learning of pupils who have witnessed and even experienced appalling conflict in their own countries. In January 2016, UNICEF published an appeal hoping to raise £806 million for the crisis in Syria, and in doing so reported on how more than 6 million children who had remained inside Syria were in vital need of humanitarian assistance, with more than 2 million children living in areas that were hard to reach or besieged (UNICEF, 2016). They also pointed to how millions of children in Syria, in addition to those children who had left Syria, had lost family members and loved ones, this in addition to losing their homes.

Children have faced almost unimaginable violence, starvation and malnutrition, and the basics such as clean water, all in addition to exploitation by adults. UNICEF (2016) also reported on how extreme weather has driven large numbers of children from their homes, rendering millions more to serious food shortages and even starvation, often resulting in violence and disease, and importantly significant risks to their education. UNICEF also reported in 2016 how some 246 million children, or one in every nine of the world's children, now live in conflict zones. UNICEF also reported that in 2015, over 16 million children were born into conflict, which was around one in every eight births.

ACTIVITY

View the following YouTube video: *Poverty: Britain's Hungry Children* (**www.youtube.com/ watch?v=ekHA8_SDwjA**), which explores the effects of austerity and poverty on children in the UK. Then consider how teachers in primary schools might support parents from very poor backgrounds in developing better nutrition for their children and improving their children's health and well-being.

POVERTY: THE CHALLENGES AHEAD FOR GROWING CHILDREN

Trainee teachers will be aware that in parts of the UK, poverty has been on the increase. An earlier publication offered by the Children's Society, *A Good Childhood for Every Child? Child Poverty in the UK* (Children's Society, 2018), made reference to the Department for Work and Pensions (DWP, 2013), which had indicated how in the UK, the 'proportion of children in poverty has risen considerably in the last 30 years – in 1979 around 14% of children lived in poverty and by 2012 it was 27%' (Children's Society, 2018, p1). The Children's Society (2011) also drew attention to the impact of economic deprivation on children's well-being. The Children's Society raised concerns that if the trend continued, governments in the UK would fail to 'meet the commitment in the Child Poverty Act to eradicate child poverty by 2020', and cited a report from the Institute for Fiscal Studies (IFS), which had estimated that a further 800,000 children would be, 'pushed into poverty by 2020 meaning one in three children in the UK will be living in poverty'. Such figures are, of course, alarming and represent challenges ahead for those preparing to enter the teaching profession.

The Children's Society (2018) also indicated how children growing up in 'low-income households are nearly three times as likely to suffer mental health problems as their more affluent peers' (p7), and cited the work of Brooks-Gunn and Duncan (1997) and Ermisch et al. (2001) to demonstrate how such children 'are more likely to suffer from low self-esteem' and also, very worryingly, 'to be socially isolated' (p7). The Children's Society has viewed the longer-term consequences of poverty as including poor health; being born prematurely and having a low birth weight and dying in their first year; having a higher rate of accidents and accidental death and, for example, being '13 times more likely to die from unintentional injury' (HM Treasury, 2008); being more likely to be absent from school because of illness or to be hospitalised; and to have long-standing illnesses and to be at risk of severe, long-term and even life-limiting illnesses. Given the nature of these statistics, it is important that trainee teachers are made aware of the potential impact that poverty can have on children's learning through poor physical health and emotional well-being. In addition, they need to fully appreciate that some of their future pupils who will have been born into very poor families may have been born prematurely and experienced difficulties in their first weeks, months and years, which may have impacted on their general development, and therefore their early learning.

— CASE STUDY 8.1

Adapting to the workplace

Judy is on her first placement as a trainee teacher in an inner-city school in an area characterised by high levels of deprivation, unemployment and crime. She has been asked to work in a Key Stage 1 class of 28 children, many of whom have grown up in families where their parents have been unemployed for years and where their parents frequently rely on food banks. Judy is told prior to her placement that there will be children in her class who are undernourished and whose parents have been registered as Class A drug users and/or alcoholics. She is pleasantly surprised on her first day to see how attentive the children are to their teacher and how much they enjoy their activities.

PARENTS' WORKING PATTERNS

Lifestyles today are in many ways vastly different to those of even a decade ago. It can be argued that many of today's parents find themselves increasingly tasked with managing lifestyles that would have been unrecognisable to their own parents, and certainly their grandparents. Many of today's young parents, for example, now start their working lives with significant amounts of debt; indeed, trainee teachers themselves will be only too well aware of the significant financial debt they accrue from student loans prior to commencing paid employment as teachers. Most everywhere one looks today, one sees examples of parents stressed by the demands of their workplace and by their perceptions, rightly or wrongly, of the need to conform to what they believe society expects of them (James, 2007). One aspect that is now recognised as contributing to stress in the lives of parents today are the expectations of their children (MacBlain, 2014), which are often derived from the media and, more recently, social media; all of this is happening at a rate that some might argue is unparalleled in our history.

How families live in the future and how parents choose to manage the lifestyles of their children will continue to change and will certainly be very different to that of today. Some young couples today may choose to put off becoming a parent until their career aspirations have been achieved or they may choose to prioritise financial security and a high standard of living before becoming a parent. Some may even choose, because of demands associated with their careers, to have only one child, with the result that their child will grow up in a home without siblings to play and interact with. Faced with the demands of the workplace, some parents may also find themselves financing activities outside of the home, which makes life easier for them as someone else is looking after and entertaining their children. Parents of children attending primary school who both work until 5.00 or 6.00 p.m. will need to organise care for their children after school as the primary school day finishes around 3.00 p.m.; teachers will need to know what is happening to their pupils either end of the school day (e.g. which pupils have been to breakfast club and who is collecting their pupils at the end of the school day).

FUTURE WORKING PATTERNS: CHALLENGES OR OPPORTUNITIES

Working patterns of parents have traditionally defined most aspects of family life; these have, of course, changed significantly over generations and will continue to do so. A major change that has impacted significantly on the lives of many children today as compared, for example, with families in the post-war years has been the increase in hours that are now being worked by both parents; in many cases, this has led to additional demands being placed on parents, and arguably mostly on mothers, who can find themselves tasked with balancing demands from their workplace with those of their families. Despite the promises of reduced working patterns and increased leisure time previously envisioned by the growth of digital technology, many parents today now find that they lead very busy and stressful lives, often characterised by long hours spent at work and the unseen demands of their workplace. How this is impacting upon the emotional and social development of young children is yet to be fully researched and understood.

Just over a decade ago, James (2007) revealed how from 1998, the number of adults in Britain who worked more than 60 hours a week had more than doubled from 10 per cent to 26 per cent. James also drew attention to how those British adults who were employed on a full-time basis were working, on average, 44 hours per week, which was the highest in the European Union (p273). Less than a decade ago, the Office for National Statistics (ONS, 2013) offered further insights into the changing nature of working patterns in the UK as follows:

> Over the past 40 years there has been a rise in the percentage of women aged 16 to 64 in employment and a fall in the percentage of men. In April to June 2013 around 67 per cent of women aged 16 to 64 were in work, an increase from 53 per cent in 1971. For men the percentage fell to 76 per cent in 2013 from 92 per cent in 1971. In April to June 2013, looking at the not seasonally adjusted series, around 13.4 million women aged 16 to 64 were in work (42 per cent part-time) and 15.3 million men (12 per cent part-time). For those who worked full-time there were differences in the average hours worked per week. For example, full-time men worked on average 44 hours per week whilst full-time women worked 40 hours per week. While there have been increases in the number of women in work, the percentage of them doing a part-time role has fluctuated between 42–45 per cent over the past 30 years.

(p1)

Of course, it needs to be emphasised that while changes in working patterns have presented difficulties for some parents and family members, they have also offered many opportunities, particularly for women. Many women in Western industrialised countries now have far greater opportunities to work and follow career paths than was the case with previous generations. Indeed, many women have experienced far greater freedom and liberty and gained rights that previously would have been considered unimaginable. Increased opportunities in education have also provided women, as well as men, with many new opportunities to improve their economic standing and that of their families, which offers additional benefits to their developing children. It must also be recognised that some parents choose to work for reasons other than financial gain (e.g. achieving long-held ambitions and opportunities to apply their creativity).

RETURNING TO WORK

Unlike other European countries, the extent of maternal employment in the UK has lagged behind. In the case of British mothers, for example, whose youngest child is aged 3–5 years, average employment rates have recently been found to be around 58 per cent, as compared to that of 64 per cent across the industrialised world (Fitzgerald and Kay, 2016). In some European countries, mothers are provided with high levels of support, which enables them to return to work more easily. In the case of Finland, for example, the majority of women have as much as a year's maternity leave and return to work after giving birth. In the case of mothers with young children who return to work in the UK, their return can be extremely challenging. In recent decades, many parents in the UK have found themselves having to earn higher incomes to meet the rising costs of living; a particular expense has been the cost of housing in some parts of the UK and the need for parents to service high mortgage repayments. The cost of housing for many young people hoping to start a family is now very expensive, which has for many parents meant a reduction in their potential work patterns, which, of course, becomes even more limited when there are the additional costs of rearing children. In some cases, parents may find they have to work significantly long hours and even have more than one job. Because households vary enormously today, it is worth emphasising how households where both parents are working and in good health are at an advantage compared with lone-parent households or households where one or both parents have poor physical and/or mental health or a disability. In all of these cases, the impact on children's emotional, physical and social well-being can be significant.

MANAGING DEVELOPMENT: WHO CARES FOR THE CHILDREN?

Many parents in the UK have traditionally relied on relatives to care for their children when they returned to work. However, with the raising of the state pension age in the UK for women to align with men, more women are now working until age 66 (or beyond), and therefore have less availability for offering support with grandchildren. Elsewhere in Europe, the picture is very different. Fitzgerald and Kay (2016, p121) have, for example, detailed some of the high levels of provision made available to mothers in Finland, emphasising how children in Finland are accorded entitlement to this provision. They emphasise how each child has a right to 'early childhood education and care' (ECEC) from birth until they are 7 years of age and that parents have this as an entitlement within two weeks of commencing work or undertaking a programme of study. Importantly, children are also provided with access to day care from birth until they are 6 years of age, usually within publicly subsidised private care settings or publicly funded care settings. From 6 years of age, children can then attend preschool for one year, during which they have a half day of early education followed by the rest of the day in day care.

Many parents in recent decades in the UK come to rely on childminders. The nature of childminding in the UK has, however, changed dramatically over recent years, with greater emphasis being placed on gaining relevant qualifications, an increased monitoring of practice through inspection, growing accountability, and a requirement to work more multi-professionally, which in some cases has meant having to work with other agencies and stakeholders (Brooker, 2016). This, combined with the initial cost of self-funded training, has resulted in a decline in registered childminders, and has shown few signs of slowing down; the decrease in numbers of registered childminders can be evidenced in the fact that in 2006, there were 71,500 childminders, while in 2010 this number dropped to 57,900, and in 2014 to 52,000 (Brind et al., 2011; Ofsted, 2014b). This trend is continuing. The benefits of children attending preschool settings was discussed more fully in Chapter 5.

— KEY THEORY

Factors in children's homes that impact on their learning: a study undertaken by Tizard and Hughes

In a celebrated study of young children's learning at home and at school, Tizard and Hughes (1984) recorded the conversations of 30 girls around the age of 4 years from two social class backgrounds (15 in each), which took place both at the children's nursery school and in their homes. The authors identified five factors originating within the children's homes that they considered to be particularly important for children's learning. These factors were as follows.

First, the very large number of activities that occurred within their homes, such as hearing telephone conversations, eating meals together, and observing visits from relatives and family friends. Through such events, children learn about their social worlds and construct their own understanding of these worlds in tandem with those around them. It is through these activities that the behaviours of others are modelled to the children, thereby facilitating and extending social learning.

Second, in their homes, 'parent and child share a common life, stretching back into the past and forward into the future' (p250), and it is this commonality of experience and life events, past and future, that helps facilitate parents' comprehension of their child's intentions. This commonality supports children with understanding and integrating new experiences into previous experiences, thereby building knowledge of the world around them, which is at the very core of their intellectual development.

Third, at the time of their study, only 11 per cent of families in Great Britain had more than two children under 16 years of age. In such families, parents were more available to their children and could spend more time engaging with them and offering quality experiences. Parents could also talk more with their children, implying that in families with a small number of children or an only child, learning could be more effective.

Fourth, 'learning is often embedded in contexts of great meaning to the child'. The nature of the close relationships within the home greatly supports children's language development as they can ask many questions while also feeling that they are being actively listened to. Tizard and Hughes referred to this as the '"curriculum" of the home', and suggested that mothers who were particu-larly close to their children typically had high expectations of them, which contributed to their children's future formal education and added positively to their children's early foundations of learning through the expectations held by their teachers.

Fifth, the 'close, and often intense' relationships found between children and their mothers. While this could hinder learning in some cases where children made excessive demands on their parents, it was suggested that the closeness to the mother ensured that children were, in fact, learning from their mother: 'It was a matter of great personal concern to most mothers in our study that their child should acquire the skills, knowledge and values that they believed to be important' (p252).

The implications of Tizard and Hughes' findings, though reported some three decades ago, take on a greater relevance for trainee teachers when consideration is given to the increased number of pupils in classrooms today whose parents may have to leave for work very early in the morning and return home sometimes in the early evening, meaning that time spent with their young children is limited.

ACTIVITY

Reflect upon your own experiences before starting primary school. Identify factors in the home that you believe supported you with later learning. Discuss with others the benefits that very young chil-dren today gain from attending preschool settings and what, if any, they lose from not being at home with a parent.

CHAPTER SUMMARY

- Today's children develop in ways that are hugely different to those of previous generations.

- Teachers working with the next generation of children will be dealing with issues that were unheard of even decades ago.

- Trainee teachers will need to continue adapting their skills and increasing their knowledge of factors affecting children's development, and importantly recognise how they themselves are also part of a rapidly changing world.

- Trainee teachers need to prepare themselves properly to work with children and families from increasingly diverse cultural backgrounds.

- Factors such as nutrition and obesity, over-sexualisation, poverty, and technology are impact-ing on and shaping children's development, and will impact on how trainee teachers work in the future with children.

SOME CONCLUDING THOUGHTS

The primary aim of this book has been to inform trainee teachers of the importance of understanding children's development and how a wide range of factors can impact on development and subsequent learning; no two children develop or learn in the same way. Children live differently today, and popularised notions of child development that have existed for many years have been radically challenged as our understanding of the impact of factors such as digital technology, social media and increased globalisation grows. We have come a long way in our understanding of children's development, and especially how emotional and social factors affect mental health and well-being in young children.

Schools in the UK now have in place policies designed to support children as they grow and develop and move through childhood and into adolescence and then early adulthood. Trainee teachers need to fully understand that every child they teach will have already commenced a learning journey, begun even before birth, that is unique to them and that has been constantly shaped by a multitude of factors and events, and by others they have come into contact with. To properly know one's pupils requires that teachers seek to understand how each pupil's unique course of development has brought them to that point where they begin to manage their learning. Trainee teachers, therefore, must themselves learn how children develop and fully appreciate how issues and events in the lives of children can impact on their development and subsequent learning; this was recently emphasised in the *Carter Review of Initial Teacher Training* (Carter, 2015).

Trainee teachers will find themselves in the future having to make important decisions about their pupils' learning and academic progress, which may even have life-changing implications for them. They will feel more confident in making such decisions if they have a sound understanding of how children develop and how development impacts on learning. Trainee teachers also need to develop their own skills in appraising learning environments and recognise that the individualised nature and ethos of schools will impact differently on individual children, and therefore their experiences of learning.

EXTENDED READING

Action for Children (2018) *Mental Health*. Available at: www.actionforchildren.org.uk/what-we-do/children-young-people/mental-health/ (accessed 18 September 2018). An excellent account of the complex factors that impact on the mental health and well-being of children and young people.

Carden, C. (ed.) (2016) *Primary Teaching*. London: SAGE. A comprehensive and up-to-date text that covers a wide range of topic areas in primary education, with contributions from a large number of academics and practitioners.

REFERENCES

Action for Children (2010) *Deprivation and Risk: The Case for Early Intervention*. London: Action for Children.

Action for Children (2018) *Mental Health*. Available at: www.actionforchildren.org.uk/what-we-do/children-young-people/mental-health/ (accessed 18 September 2018).

Ansari, D., Coch, D. and De Smedt, B. (2011) 'Connecting education and cognitive neuroscience: where will the journey take us?' *Educational Philosophy and Theory*, 43(1): 37–42.

ARK (2014) *Queering the Family: Attitudes towards Lesbian and Gay Relationships and Families in Northern Ireland*. Belfast: NILT.

Arnott, L. (2016) 'The role of digital technologies', in I. Palaiologou (ed.), *The Early Years Foundation Stage: Theory and Practice* (3rd edn). London: SAGE.

Bailey, R. (2011) *Letting Children Be Children: Report of an Independent Review of the Commercialization and Sexualization of Childhood*. London: Department for Education.

Bandura, A. (1977a) *Self-Efficacy: The Exercise of Control*. New York: Freeman.

Bandura, A. (1977b) *Social Learning Theory*. Englewood Cliffs, NJ: Prentice Hall.

Barnard, P., Morland, I. and Nagy, J. (1999) *Children, Bereavement and Trauma: Nurturing Resilience*. London: Jessica Kingsley.

Bending, H. (2018) 'Resilience in childhood', in I. Luke and J. Gourd (eds), *Thriving as a Professional Teacher*. London: Routledge.

Bennett, T. (2017) *Creating a Culture: How School Leaders Can Optimise Behaviour. Independent Review of Behaviour in Schools*. London: Department for Education.

Bigge, M.L. and Shermis, S.S. (2004) *Learning Theories for Teachers* (6th edn). Boston, MA: Pearson.

Boon, M. (2010) *Understanding Dyspraxia: A Guide for Parents and Teachers* (2nd edn). London: Jessica Kingsley.

Brind, R., Norden, O., McGinigal, S., Garnett, E., Oseman, D., La Valle, I. and Jelicic, H. (2011) *Childcare and Early Years Providers*. London: Department for Education.

Bronfenbrenner, U. (1979) *Ecology of Human Development*. Cambridge, MA: Harvard University Press.

Brooker, L. (2016) 'Childminders, parents and policy: testing the triangle of care', *Journal of Early Childhood Research*, 14(1): 69–83.

Brooks, V., Abbott, I. and Bills, L. (2004) *Preparing to Teach in Secondary Schools*. Maidenhead: Open University Press.

Brooks-Gunn, J. and Duncan, G. (1997) 'The effects of poverty on children', *The Future of Children*, 7(2): 55–71.

Brown, A. (1994) 'The advancement of learning', *Educational Researcher*, 23: 4–12.

Brown, G. (1977) *Child Development*. Shepton Mallet: Open Books.

Bruner, J. (1975) 'Language as an instrument in thought', in A. Davies (ed.), *Problems of Language and Learning*. London: Heinemann.

Buckingham, D. (2000) *After the Death of Childhood: Growing up in the Age of Electronic Media*. Cambridge: Polity Press.

Buckler, S. and Castle, P. (2014) *Psychology for Teachers*. London: SAGE.

Burden, R.L. (1987) 'Feuerstein's instrumental enrichment programme: important issues in research and evaluation', *European Journal of Psychology of Education*, 2(1): 3–16.

Carter, A. (2015) *Carter Review of Initial Teacher Training*. Available at: www.gov.uk/government/publications/carter-review-of-initial-teacher-training (accessed 28 August 2018).

Carter, C. and Nutbrown, C. (2014) 'The tools of assessment: watching and learning', in G. Pugh and B. Duffy (eds), *Contemporary Issues in the Early Years*. London: SAGE.

Case, R. (1998) 'Changing views of knowledge and their impact on educational research and practice', in D. Olsen and N. Torrance (eds), *Handbook of Education and Human Development*. Malden, MA: Blackwell.

Castrén, A. and Widmer, E. (2015) 'Insiders and outsiders in stepfamilies: adults' and children's views on family boundaries', *Current Sociology*, 63(1): 36–56.

Cawson, P. (2002) *Child Maltreatment in the Family*. London: National Society for the Prevention of Cruelty to Children.

Chedzoy, S.M. and Burden, R.L. (2005) 'Making the move: assessing student attitudes to primary secondary transfer', *Research in Education*, 74(1): 22–35.

Children's Society (2011) *How Happy Are Our Children: Measuring Children's Well-Being and Exploring Economic Factors*. London: Children's Society.

Children's Society (2018) *A Good Childhood for Every Child? Child Poverty in the UK*. Available at: www.childrenssociety.org.uk/sites/default/files/tcs/2013_child_poverty_briefing_1.pdf (accessed 20 December 2018).

CHILDWISE (2015) *The Monitor Pre-School Report: Key Behaviour Patterns Among 0–4 Year Olds*. London: CHILDWISE.

Choi, K. (2012) 'Supporting transition from primary to secondary school using the Protective Behaviours programme', *Educational & Child Psychology*, 29(3): 27–37.

Clark, L. (2012) 'Nurseries label one-year-olds "special needs"', *Daily Mail*, 13 July, p12.

Claxton, G. (2005) *An Intelligent Look at Emotional Intelligence*. London: Association of Teachers and Lecturers.

Cobb, P. (1994) 'Where is the mind? Constructivist and sociocultural perspectives on mathematical development', *Educational Researcher*, 23(7): 13–20.

Colverd, S. and Hodgkin, B. (2011) *Developing Emotional Intelligence in the Primary School*. London: Routledge.

Cowie, H. (2012) *From Birth to Sixteen: Children's Health, Social, Emotional and Linguistic Development*. London: Routledge.

Craft, A. (2012) 'Childhood in a digital age: creative challenges for educational futures', *London Review of Education*, 10(2): 173–90.

Crafter, S. and Maunder, R. (2012) 'Understanding transitions using a sociocultural framework', *Educational and Child Psychology*, 29(1): 10–17.

Cregan, K. and Cuthbert, D. (2014) *Global Childhoods*. London: SAGE.

Crowley, K. (2014) *Child Development: A Practical Introduction*. London: SAGE.

Cullis, A. and Hansen, K. (2009) *Child Development in the First Three Sweeps of the Millennium Cohort Study*. *DCSF Research Report RW-007*. London: Department for Children, Schools and Families.

Curran, A. (2012) 'Autism and the brain's working: how far have we got?', *Debate*, 144: 5–6.

Currie, C., Roberts, C. and Morgan, A. (2008) *Health Behaviour in School-Aged Children: International Report from 2005/2006 Study*. Geneva: World Health Organization.

Cuthbert, C., Rayns, G. and Stanley, K. (2011) *All Babies Count: Prevention and Protection for Vulnerable Babies. A Review of the Evidence.* London: National Society for the Prevention of Cruelty to Children.

CYPMHC (2012) *Resilience and Results: How to Improve the Emotional and Mental Wellbeing of Children and Young People in Your School.* London: Children and Young People's Mental Health Coalition.

Daniels, D.H. and Shumow, L. (2002) 'Child development and classroom teaching: a review of the literature and implications for educating teachers', *Applied Developmental Psychology*, 23: 495–526.

Daudelin, M. (1996) 'Learning from experience through reflection', *Dynamics*, 24(3): 36–48.

DfE (2012) *QTS Teachers' Standards.* London: Department for Education.

DfE (2015) *Early Years Foundation Stage Profile Results in England, 2015.* London: Department for Education.

DfES (2008) *Statutory Framework for the Early Years Foundation Stage.* Nottingham: DfES.

Dunn, J. (2015) 'Insiders' perspectives: a children's rights approach to involving children in advising on adult-initiated research', *International Journal of Early Years Education*, 23(4): 394–408.

DWP (2013) *Households Below Average Income 2011/2012.* London: Department for Work and Pensions.

Elkind, D. (1981) *The Hurried Child: Growing Up Too Fast Too Soon.* Reading, MA: Perseus Publishing.

Erikson, E. (1980) *Identity and Life Cycle.* New York: Norton.

Ermisch, J., Francesconi, M. and Pevalin, D. (2001) *Outcomes for Children of Poverty.* London: Department for Work and Pensions.

Fausto-Sterling, A. (2000) *Sexing the Body: Gender Politics and the Construction of Sexuality.* New York: Basic Books.

Fenton, B. (2006) 'Junk culture "is poisoning our children"', *Daily Telegraph*, 12 September, p1.

Feuerstein, R., Rand, Y., Hoffman, M.B. and Miller, R. (1980) *Instrumental Enrichment: An Intervention Programme for Cognitive Modifiability.* Baltimore, MD: University Park Press.

Field, F. (2010) *The Foundation Years: Preventing Poor Children Becoming Poor Adults. Report of the Independent Review on Poverty and Life Chances.* London: Cabinet Office.

Fitzgerald, D. and Kay, J. (2016) *Understanding Early Years Policy* (4th edn). London: SAGE.

Fontana, D. (1995) *Psychology for Teachers* (3rd edn). Basingstoke: Macmillan Press.

Gardner, H. (1983) *Frames of Mind.* London: Fontana.

Garmezy, N. (1985) 'Stress resilient children: the search for protective factors', in J. Stevenson (ed.), *Recent Research in Developmental Psychopathogy.* Oxford: Pergamon Press.

Gautier, A., Wellard, S. and Cardy, S. (2013) *Forgotten Children: Children Growing Up in Kinship Care.* London: Grandparents Plus.

Goleman, D. (1996) *Emotional Intelligence: Why It Can Matter More Than IQ.* London: Bloomsbury.

Good Schools Guide (2013a) *Educating the Gifted Child.* Available at: www.goodschoolsguide.co.uk/help-and-advice/your-child/gifted-talented-able-children/439/educating-the-gifted-child (accessed 5 March 2013).

Good Schools Guide (2013b) *The Gifted Child.* Available at: www.goodschoolsguide.co.uk/help-and-advice/your-child/gifted-talented-able-children/214/the-gifted-child (accessed 5 March 2013).

GOV.UK (2011) *Advancing Transgender Equality: A Plan for Action.* Available at: www.gov.uk/government/publications/transgender-action-plan (accessed 5 August 2019).

GOV.UK (2015) *Record Number of Children Adopted by LGBT Families.* Available at: www.gov.uk/government/news/record-number-of-children-adopted-by-lgbt-families (accessed 5 August 2019).

Gray, C. and MacBlain, S.F. (2015) *Learning Theories in Childhood* (2nd edn). London: SAGE.

Green, M. and Kerr, B. (2019) 'What drives primary schools today?', in C. Carden (ed.), *Primary Teaching.* London: SAGE.

Gross, R.D. (1992) *Psychology: The Science of Mind and Behaviour* (2nd edn). London: Hodder & Stoughton.

Grotberg, E. (1995) *A Guide to Promoting Resilience in Children*. The Hague: Bernard van Leer Foundation.

Hardy, M. and Heyes, S. (1994) *Beginning Psychology: A Comprehensive Introduction to Psychology* (4th edn). Oxford: Oxford University Press.

Hattie, J. (2008) *Visible Learning: A Synthesis of Over 800 Meta-Analyses Relating to Achievement*. London: Routledge.

Hattie, J. (2012) *Visible Learning for Teachers: Maximising Impact on Learning*. London: Routledge.

Hattie, J. and Yates, G.C.R. (2014) *Visible Learning and the Science of How We Learn*. London: SAGE.

Hayes, N. (1994) *Foundations of Psychology: An Introductory Text*. London: Routledge.

Hayward, L. and Hayward, S. (2016) 'Assessment and learning', in D. Wyse and S. Rogers (eds), *A Guide to Early Years and Primary Teaching*. London: SAGE.

Heath, S. (1983) *Ways with Words: Language, Life and Work in Communities and Classrooms*. New York: Cambridge University Press.

Hegde, A.V., Averett, P., White, C.P. and Deese, S. (2014) 'Examining preschool teachers' attitudes, comfort, action orientation and preparation to work with children reared by gay and lesbian parents', *Early Child Development and Care*, 184(7): 963–76.

Hicks, D. (2004) 'The global dimension in the curriculum', in S. Ward (ed.), *Education Studies: A Student's Guide*. London: RoutledgeFalmer.

HM Treasury (2008) *Ending Child Poverty*. London: HM Treasury.

Hohnen, B. and Murphy, T. (2016) 'The optimum context for learning: drawing on neuroscience to inform best practice in the classroom', *Educational & Child Psychology*, 33(1): 75–90.

Hope, S. (2018) 'Principled professionalism in the classroom', in I. Luke and J. Gourd (eds), *Thriving as a Professional Teacher*. London: Routledge.

Howard-Jones, P. (2014) *Neuroscience and Education: A Review of Educational Interventions and Approaches Informed by Neuroscience*. Bristol: Education Endowment Foundation, University of Bristol.

HSCIC (2015) *Statistics on Obesity, Physical Activity and Diet: England 2015*. Available at: http://digital.nhs.uk/catalogue/PUB16988/obes-phys-acti-diet-eng-2015.pdf (accessed 16 August 2019).

Infed (2018) *Caring in Education*. Available at: http://infed.org/mobi/caring-in-education/ (accessed 16 October 2018).

Isaacs, S. (1929) *The Nursery Years*. London: Routledge.

Isaacs, S. (1930) *Intellectual Growth in Young Children*. London: Routledge.

Isaacs, S. (1932) *The Children We Teach*. London: University of London Press.

Jadue-Roa, D.S. and Whitebread, D. (2012) 'Young children's experiences through transition between kindergarten and first grade in Chile and its relation with their developing learning agency', *Educational & Child Psychology*, 29(1): 32–46.

James, O. (2007) *Affluenza*. London: Vermillion.

Jarvis, M. (2005) *The Psychology of Effective Learning and Teaching*. Cheltenham: Nelson Thornes.

Jütte, S., Bentley, H., Tallis, D., Mayes, J., Jetha, N., O'Hagan, O., et al. (2015) *How Safe Are Our Children? The Most Comprehensive Overview of Child Protection in the UK*. London: National Society for the Prevention of Cruelty to Children.

Kennedy, E., Cameron, R.J. and Greene, J. (2012) Transitions in the early years: educational and child psychologists working to reduce the impact of school culture shock, *Educational & Child Psychology*, 29(1): 19–30.

Kintner-Duffy, V.L., Vardell, R., Lower, J.K. and Cassidy, D. (2012) 'The changers and the changed: preparing early childhood teachers to work with lesbian, gay, bisexual and transgender families', *Journal of Early Childhood Teacher Education*, 33(3): 208–23.

Knowles, G. (2013) 'Families, identity and cultural heritage', in G. Knowles and R. Holmström (eds), *Understanding Family Diversity and Home–School Relations*. London: Routledge.

Knowles, G. and Holmström, R. (2013) *Understanding Family Diversity and Home–School Relations*. London: Routledge.

Kohlberg, L. (1981) *Essays on Moral Development*. New York: Harper & Row.

Kokkinaki, T. and Vasdekis, V.G.S. (2015) 'Comparing emotional coordination in early spontaneous mother–infant and father–infant interactions', *European Journal of Developmental Psychology*, 12(1): 69–84.

Kring, A., Johnson, S., Davison, G., Neale, J., Edelstyn, N. and Brown, D. (2013) *Abnormal Psychology* (12th edn). Singapore: John Wiley & Sons.

Linden, J. (2005) *Understanding Child Development: Linking Theory to Practice*. London: Hodder Education.

Lundy, L. (2007) 'Voice is not enough: conceptualizing Article 12 of the United Nations Convention on the Rights of the Child', *British Educational Research Journal*, 33(6): 927–942.

Lundy, L. and McEvoy, L. (2009) 'Developing outcomes for educational services: a children's rights-based approach', *Effective Education*, 1(1): 43–60.

Lundy, L., McEvoy, L. and Byrne, B. (2011) 'Working with young children as co-researchers: an approach informed by the United Nations Convention on the Rights of the Child', *Early Education and Development*, 22(5): 714–736.

Lyons, R. and Woods, K. (2012) 'Effective transition to secondary school for shy, less confident children: a case study using "pyramid" group work', *Educational & Child Psychology*, 29(3): 8–26.

MacBlain, S.F. (2014) *How Children Learn*. London: SAGE.

MacBlain, S.F. (2018) *Learning Theories for Early Years Practice*. London: SAGE.

MacBlain, S.F. (2019) 'How do children learn?', in C. Carden (ed.), *Primary Teaching*. London: SAGE.

MacBlain, S.F. and MacBlain, M.S. (2004) 'Addressing the needs of lone-parent pupils', *Academic Exchange Quarterly*, 8(2): 221–5.

MacBlain, S.F. and Purdy, N. (2010) 'Confidence or confusion: how prepared are today's NQTs to meet the additional needs of children in schools?', *Journal of Teacher Development*, 3(15): 381–94.

MacBlain, S.F., Dunn, J. and Luke, I. (2017) *Contemporary Childhood*. London: SAGE.

MacBlain, S.F., Long, L. and Dunn, J. (2015) *Dyslexia, Literacy and Inclusion: Child-Centred Perspectives*. London: SAGE.

Macintyre, C. (2002) *Play for Children with Special Needs: Including Children Aged 3–8*. London: David Fulton.

Macintyre, C. and McVitty, K. (2004) *Movement and Learning in the Early Years: Supporting Dyspraxia (DCD) and Other Difficulties*. London: Paul Chapman.

Marsh, J. (2004) 'The techno-literacy practices of young children', *Journal of Early Childhood Research*, 2(1): 51–66.

Marsh, J., Plowman, L., Yamada-Rice, D., Bishop, J.C., Lahmar, J., Scott, F., et al. (2015) *Exploring Play and Creativity in Pre-Schoolers' Use of Apps: Report for Early Years Practitioners*. Available at: http://techandplay.org/tap-media-pack.pdf (accessed 7 August 2019).

Marzano, R. (2005) *School Leadership That Works: From Research to Results*. Alexandria, VA: ASCD.

Marzano, R. (2007) *The Art and Science of Teaching: A Comprehensive Framework for Effective Instruction*. Alexandria, VA: ASCD.

Marzano, R. and Kendall, J.S. (2006) *The New Taxonomy of Educational Objectives* (2nd edn). Thousand Oaks, CA: SAGE.

McDowall Clark, R. (2010) *Childhood in Society: For Early Childhood Studies*. Exeter: Learning Matters.

McMillan, D. (2009) 'Preparing for educare: student perspectives on early years training in Northern Ireland', *International Journal of Early Years Education*, 17(3): 219–35.

Mental Health Foundation (2018) *Mental Health in Children and Young People*. Available at: www.mental-health.org.uk/a-to-z/c/children-and-young-people (accessed 18 September 2018).

Mercer, J. (2018) *Child Development: Concepts and Theories*. London: SAGE.

Miller, L. and Pound, L. (2011) *Theories and Approaches to Learning in the Early Years*. London: SAGE.

Moll, L. and Greenberg, J. (1988) 'Creating zones of possibilities: combining social contexts for instruction', in L. Moll (ed.), *Vygotsky and Education: Instrumental Implications and Applications of Sociohistorical Psychology*. New York: Cambridge University Press.

Moore, S. and Rosenthal, D. (2006) *Sexuality in Adolescence: Current Trends*. London: Routledge.

Mundy, K. (1998) 'Educational multilaterialism and world (dis)order', *Comparative Education Review*, 42(4): 448–78.

NALDIC (2012) *Research and Information*. Available at: www.naldic.org.uk/research-and-information/eal-statistics/eal-pupils (accessed 16 August 2019).

NCB (2016) *Children's Grief Awareness Week: 40,000 Children Bereaved of a Parent Each Year*. Available at: www.ncb.org.uk/news/childrens-grief-awareness-week-40000-children-bereaved-of-a-parent-each-year (accessed 30 March 2016).

Neill, A.S. (1968) *Summerhill*. Harmondsworth: Pelican.

Niner, S., Ahmed, Y. and Cuthbert, D. (2013) 'The "social tsunami": media coverage of child abuse in Malaysia's English-language newspapers in 2010', *Media, Culture & Society*, 35(4): 435–53.

NSPCC (2014) *What's Affecting Children in 2013: Can I Tell You Something Childline Review 2012/13*. London: National Society for the Prevention of Cruelty to Children.

Nutbrown, C. (2006a) *Threads of Thinking: Young Children Learning and the Role of Early Education*. London: SAGE.

Nutbrown, C. (2006b) 'Watching and listening: the tools of assessment', in G. Pugh and B. Duffy (eds), *Contemporary Issues in the Early Years*. London: SAGE.

Ofcom (2014) *Children and Parents: Media Use and Attitudes Report*. Available at: http://stakeholders.ofcom.org.uk/market-data-research/other/research-publications/childrens/children-parents-oct-14/ (accessed 7 August 2019).

Ofsted (2010) *Learning: Creative Approaches That Raise Standards*. London: Office for Standards in Education.

Ofsted (2011) *Removing Barriers to Literacy*. London: Office for Standards in Education.

Ofsted (2013a) *The Most Able Students: Are They Doing as Well as They Should in Our Non-Selective Secondary Schools?* London: Office for Standards in Education.

Ofsted (2013b) *What About the Children? Joint Working between Adult and Children's Services When Parents or Carers Have Mental Ill Health and/or Drug and Alcohol Problems*. Manchester: Office for Standards in Education.

Ofsted (2014a) *Are You Ready? Good Practice in School Readiness*. Manchester: Office for Standards in Education.

Ofsted (2014b) *Registered Childcare Providers and Places in England, August 2014: Key Findings*. London: Office for Standards in Education.

Ofsted (2015) *The Report of Her Majesty's Chief Inspector of Education, Children's Services and Skills 2013–14 Social Care*. Manchester: Office for Standards in Education.

Ofsted (2017) *Bold Beginnings: The Reception Curriculum in a Sample of Good and Outstanding Primary Schools*. Manchester: Office for Standards in Education.

Olson, D. and Bruner, J. (1996) 'Folk psychology and fold pedagogy', in D. Olson and N. Torrance (eds), *Handbook of Education and Development: New Models of Learning, Teaching, and Schooling*. Malden, MA: Blackwell.

ONS (2013) *Women in the Labour Market*. Available at: www.ons.gov.uk/ons/dcp171776_328352.pdf (accessed 20 January 2015).

ONS (2015) *Families and Households 2014*. Available at: www.ons.gov.uk/ons/dcp171778_393133.pdf (accessed 5 August 2019).

Palaiologou, I. (2019) 'What do student teachers need to know about child development?', in C. Carden (ed.), *Primary Teaching*. London: SAGE.

Palmer, S. (2006) *Toxic Childhood*. London: Orion.

Papatheodorou, T. and Potts, D. (2016) 'Pedagogy in practice', in I. Palaiologou (ed.), *The Early Years Foundation Stage: Theory and Practice* (3rd edn). London: SAGE.

Paton, G. (2012) 'New-style "nappy curriculum" will damage childhood', *The Telegraph*, 6 February. Available at: www.telegraph.co.uk/education/educationnews/9064870/New-style-nappy-curriculum-will-damage-childhood.html (accessed 7 August 2019).

Piaget, J.P. (1952) *The Origins of Intelligence in Children*. New York: International Universities Press.

Rigby, E. (2016) 'Teenagers' sexting out of control, says Labour', *The Times*, 22 March, p13.

Roffey, S. (2016) 'Building a case for whole-child, whole-school wellbeing in challenging contexts', *Educational & Child Psychology*, 33(2): 30–42.

Rose, J. and Wood, F. (2016) 'Child development', in D. Wyse and S. Rogers (eds), *A Guide to Early Years and Primary Teaching*. London: SAGE.

Ross, N.J., Church, S., Hill, M., Seaman, P. and Roberts, T. (2012) 'The perspectives of young men and their teenage partners on maternity and health services during pregnancy and early parenthood', *Children in Society*, 26: 304–15.

Rutter, M. (2006) 'Implications of resilience concepts for scientific understanding', *Annals of the New York Academy of Sciences*, 1094: 1–12.

Sadowski, C. and McIntosh. J. (2016) 'On laughter and loss: children's views of shared time, parenting and security post separation', *Childhood*, 23(1): 69–86.

Salovey, P. and Mayer, J.D. (1990) 'Emotional intelligence', *Imagination, Cognition and Personality*, 9(3): 185–211.

Sarkadi, A., Kristiansson, R., Oberklaid, F. and Bremberg, S. (2008) 'Fathers' involvement and children's developmental outcomes: a systematic review of longitudinal studies', *Acta Paediatrica*, 97(2): 153–8.

Save the Children (2018) *Early Language Development and Children's Primary School Attainment in English and Maths: New Research Findings*. Available at: www.savethechildren.org.uk/content/dam/global/reports/education-and-child-protection/early_language_development_briefing_paper.pdf (accessed 22 September 2018).

Senior, J. (2016) *Broken and Betrayed: The True Story of the Rotherham Abuse Scandal by the Woman Who Fought to Expose It*. London: Pan Books.

Siberfield, C. (2016) 'Children's health and well-being', in I. Palaiologou (ed.), *The Early Years Foundation Stage: Theory and Practice* (3rd edn). London: SAGE.

Skinner, B.F. (1951) *How to Teach Animals*. San Francisco, CA: W.H. Freeman.

Skinner, B.F. (1953) *Science and Human Behavior*. New York: Simon & Schuster.

Sorin, R. (2005) 'Changing images of childhood: reconceptualising early childhood practice', *International Journal of Transitions in Childhood*, 1: 12–21.

Stanford, P. (2012) 'Can 20% of school children really have special needs?', *Daily Telegraph*, 12 May, p23.

Steinberg, S.R. and Kincheloe, J.L. (eds) (2004) *Kinderculture: The Corporate Construction of Childhood* (2nd edn). Oxford: Westview Press.

Sylvester, R. and Thompson, A. (2016) 'Children grow up watching porn and think it's normal', *The Times*, 22 March, p12.

Taggart, B., Sylva, K., Melhuish, E., Sammons, P. and Siraj, I. (2015) *Effective Pre-School, Primary and Secondary Education Project (EPPSE 3-16+): How Pre-School Influences Children and Young People's Attainment and Developmental Outcomes over Time Research Brief June 2015*. Available at: https://assets.publishing.service.gov.uk/government/uploads/system/uploads/attachment_data/file/455670/RB455_Effective_pre-school_primary_and_secondary_education_project.pdf.pdf (accessed 31 December 2018).

Tizard, B. and Hughes, M. (1984) *Young Children Learning: Learning and Thinking at Home and at School*. London: Fontana.

Tobell, J. (2003) 'Students' experiences of the transition from primary to secondary school', *Educational and Child Psychology*, 20(4): 4–14.

UNICEF (2016) *UNICEF Appeals for £806 Million for Syria Crisis Response: Alarming Figures Highlight Extent of Humanitarian Crisis*. Available at: www.unicef.org.uk/Media-centre/Press-releases/Unicef-appeals-for-806-million-for-Syria-crisis-response-alarming-figures-highlight-extent-of-humanitarian-crisis/ (accessed 2 February 2016).

Vygotsky, L. (1978) *Mind in Society: The Development of Higher Psychological Processes*. Cambridge, MA: Harvard University Press.

Vygotsky, L. (2002) *Language and Thought* (ed. and rev. A. Kozulin). Cambridge, MA: MIT Press.

Walker, A., Flatley, J. and Kershaw, C. (eds) (2009) *Crime in England and Wales 2008/09. Vol. 1: Findings from the British Crime Survey and Police Recorded Crime*. London: HMSO.

Walsh, G. (2017) 'Why playful teaching and learning?', in G. Walsh, D. McMillan and C. McGuinness (eds), *Playful Teaching and Learning*. London: SAGE.

Watson, J.B. (1928) *Psychological Care of Infant and Child*. New York: Norton.

Whitebread, D. (2012) *Developmental Psychology and Early Childhood Education*. London: SAGE.

Whitebread, D. and Sinclair-Harding, L. (2014) 'Neuroscience and the infant brain', *Nursery World*, 20 October–2 November, 21–4.

WHO (2002) *World Health Report: Reducing Risks, Promoting Healthy Life*. Geneva: World Health Organization.

WHO (2015) *Facts and Figures on Childhood Obesity*. Available at: www.who.int/end-childhood-obesity/facts/en/ (accessed 30 October 2015).

WHO (2016) *Report of the Commission on Ending Childhood Obesity (ECHO)*. Available at: www.who.int/end-childhood-obesity/final-report/en/ (accessed 30 March 2016).

Wilshaw, M. (2014) *Unsure Start: HMCI's Early Years Annual Report 2012/13 Speech 2014*.

Zwozdiak-Mayers, P. (ed.) (2007) *Childhood and Youth Studies*. Exeter: Learning Matters.

INDEX